Contents

© 1997 Abingdon Press.

Illustrated by:
• Robert S. Jones

D1226086

Contributing \
• Daphna L. Flegal, M. A.
• Charles R. Foster, Ed.D
• Susan M. Isbell, M.A.
• James H. Ritchie, Jr., Ed.D
• LeeDell B. Stickler, M. A.

Baptism & Communion

Supplies

- Bible
- hymnals
- CD
- plastic dishpan, tub, or bowl
- crayons, markers, pencils
- glue, clear tape, masking tape, tacks
- stapler, staples
- construction paper
- tissue paper
- file folders
- envelopes
- plain paper
- tempera paint
- scissors
- posterboard, bubble wrap, or sandpaper
- mural paper
- plastic tablecloths or beach towels
- paper punch
- yarn
- coverups
- towels
- paper cups
- water
- pretzels, crackers
- napkins
- plastic containers
- newspapers
- large and small paper bags
- food coloring
- paper towels

- coffee filters
- paper plates
- glitter or glitter glue
- box lids, trays, shallow trays
- large plastic pitcher or container
- bread basket
- different kinds of bread
- cookie dough, colored sugar or candy sprinkles, flour, rolling pins, cookie sheets
- bottle of grape juice
- cheese, grapes, dates, figs or fig cookies, olives, pomegranates
- Communion items
- craft sticks or tongue depressors
- canned or frozen bread dough, or ingredients for bread dough
- honey, butter, or jam
- measuring cups and spoons
- mixing bowl, large spoon, 13-by-9-inch pan
- ingredients for blue finger gelatin
- cooking utensils
- platters
- tablespoons
- table knives or plastic knives

- baptism certificates, photographs, baptismal gowns
- scarf or bandanna
- pastor's stole
- white burlap, large white cloth
- clear plastic cups (two sizes)
- purple ribbon
- drinking straws
- cotton swabs
- cleanup supplies
- meat hammer, cutting board, barley
- candles, matches
- white feathers
- colored cellophane
- blue crepe paper
- four sponges
- small plastic pitcher
- watercolor brushes
- colored tissue paper strips
- CD player
- Communion cups
- plastic grapes
- white felt
- purple felt
- optional: umbrella, Bible-times costumes, fabric paints, sequins, jewels, braid, plastic dove

Scriptures for Baptism
Matthew 3:13-17; Mark 1:9-11; Luke 3:21-22; John 1:29-34

Understanding the Bible Verses

John, often known as John the Baptist, was the son of Elizabeth and Zechariah. He was a relative of Jesus and probably had known Jesus all his life. The ministry of John the Baptist set the stage for the baptism of Jesus. John had become a charismatic preacher, working in the Judean wilderness. He preached repentance and baptized people with water as a sign of forgiveness. The symbolic cleansing by water helped the people understand that God had washed away their old sinful lives.

Jesus came to John as one of the crowd, as one of those who was coming to God. While Jesus did not need to confess sins in order to be baptized, his submission to the same baptism as those around him symbolized the beginning of his public ministry, and also identified him closely with those he came to save.

The dove is symbolic of the Holy Spirit. It is significant to our understanding of the sacrament because it shows that baptism is not merely an action on our part. It is important to remember that God is the primary actor in the sacrament of baptism. Baptism is a time when we receive the Holy Spirit as we are claimed by God.

Understanding Your Children

Baptism is an outward symbol of God's action in our lives. It is one way we publicly acknowledge God's claim on us and recognize God's love for us. As baptized people, we attempt to live as God plans for us to live. We seek to follow the teachings of Jesus and to share the story of Jesus with others.

Early elementary children are still concrete thinkers. They may not understand the abstract symbolism of baptism. They may have a difficult time identifying with something they cannot see or hear or feel in the physical sense. Help the children understand baptism as a way we celebrate that we belong to God.

Children in first, second, and third grades are beginning to identify themselves with groups of friends. This need to belong continues as the children grow. It can be reassuring for children to know that they belong to God and are a part of the family of God, the church. Do not let the children feel awkward if they have not been baptized yet. It is important for all children, whether they have been baptized or not, to know that God loves them, that they are children of God, and that they belong to God. Encourage the children to talk with their parents if they feel the time is right for them to be baptized.

Developing Your Faith

Read Matthew 3:13-17; Mark 1:9-11; Luke 3:21-22; and John 1:29-34. Compare the stories of Jesus' baptism as they are written in the four Gospels. The Matthew, Mark, and Luke verses all testify that Jesus is God's beloved son. Through Jesus you are a beloved child of God. God is well-pleased with you, not because of anything you have done or have not done, but because you are simply you.

Read Matthew 3:13-17. Water is a life-giving symbol when it is used in baptism. Remember your baptism and the promises that were made when you were publicly identified as a child of God. If you have a hymnal available, read the ritual for baptism. How is God calling you to live out your baptism?

Read Mark 1:9-11. When Jesus was baptized, he was empowered by the Holy Spirit to begin his ministry. Do you see evidence of the Holy Spirit at work in your life? Pray that the Holy Spirit will empower you in your ministry with children. Pray for each of your children by name.

Baptism

God said, "You are my own dear Son. I am pleased with you."
(Mark 1:11, *Good News Bible*, adapted)

Lesson Overview

✓ Learning Experiences	✓ Supplies	✓ Before Class
Who's Who	CD, CD player, nametags *(page 10)*, blue crayons, paper punch, scissors, yarn or tape, marker	Photocopy and cut out nametags.
Water Drops	coffee filters or paper towels, scissors, yarn, food coloring, water, plastic containers, newspapers, paper punch, coverups (optional: tape, umbrella)	
Water Works	water, plastic tablecloths or beach towels, buckets or cans, tablespoons, towels	
Sing 'n Swing	CD, CD player, hymnals	
Hand 'n Hand Bible Story	"Jesus Is God's Son" story *(page 5)*	
Touch the Water	CD, CD player, sponge, Bible, bowl or dishpan, water, paper towels	
Splash 'n Sing	CD, CD player, *page 14*	
Baptism Booklets	black construction paper, blue tissue or construction paper, scissors, paper punch, glue, file folders	
Visit the Baptismal Font	Bible, Bible verse *(page 11)*, baptism certificate, baptism photos, baptismal gown, baptism booklets	Photocopy Bible verse.
Sing a Blessing	CD, CD player, hymnals	
Share a Salty Snack	salty pretzels or crackers, napkins, paper cups, water, plastic pitcher	
Time to Go	letter to parents *(page 12)*, baptism questionnaire *(page 13)*, envelopes	Photocopy letter to parents and baptism questionnaire.

Jesus Is God's Son

by Daphna Flegal and LeeDell Stickler

"Come," shouted John the Baptist. "Come and hear about God's son." John talked to the people by the side of the Jordan River. He told people the good news about God's son.

God's son. God's son.
(Cross left hand over right hand two times. Cross right hand over left hand two times.)
Jesus is the one.
(Pat hands on knees twice; point index finger and move hand forward.)
God's son. God's son.
(Cross left hand over right hand two times. Cross right hand over left hand two times.)
Jesus is God's son.
(Pat knees twice; cross hands over chest.)

"Tell God you are sorry for the wrong things you have done," John said. "Let me baptize you."

The people came to the river to be baptized. They heard John tell the good news about God's son.

God's son. God's son.
(Cross left hand over right hand two times. Cross right hand over left hand two times.)
Jesus is the one.
(Pat hands on knees twice; point index finger and move hand forward.)
God's son. God's son.
(Cross left hand over the right hand two times. Cross right hand over the left hand two times.)
Jesus is God's son.
(Pat knees twice; cross hands over chest.)

"Are you the one?" the people asked John. "Are you the Messiah?"

"No," answered John. "I am not the one. I am only the messenger. I baptize you with water. The one who is coming will baptize you with the Holy Spirit."

God's son. God's son.
(Cross left hand over right hand two times. Cross right hand over left hand two times.)
Jesus is the one.
(Pat hands on knees twice; point index finger and move hand forward.)
God's son. God's son.
(Cross left hand over right hand two times. Cross right hand over left hand two times.)
Jesus is God's son.
(Pat knees twice; cross hands over chest.)

One day Jesus came to the Jordan River. "I want you to baptize me," Jesus said to John. Jesus walked into the water of the Jordan River. John baptized Jesus with the water. When Jesus came out of the water of the river, Jesus saw a dove flying in the sky. Jesus heard God's voice.

God said, "You are my own dear Son. I am pleased with you." Jesus was the one. Jesus was God's son.

God's son. God's son.
(Cross left hand over right hand two times. Cross right hand over left hand two times.)
Jesus is the one.
(Pat hands on knees twice; point index finger and move hand forward.)
God's son. God's son.
(Cross left hand the right hand two times. Cross right hand over left hand two times.)
Jesus is God's son.
(Pat knees twice; cross hands over chest.)

(Based on Mark 1:9-11.)

Who's Who

CD, CD player, nametags *(page 10)*, blue crayons, marker, paper punch, scissors, yarn or tape

- Play "Water Sounds" from the **CD** as the children arrive. Greet each child by name. If you do not know the children's names, make nametags.

- Photocopy the nametags with the water pictures *(page 10)*. Let the children cut the nametags apart. Have each child color a nametag with a blue crayon and then write her or his name on the nametag with a marker. Let the child use a paper punch to make a hole in the top of the nametag. Measure a length of yarn to fit easily over the child's head. Have each child thread the yarn through the hole and tie the ends of the yarn together to make a nametag necklace. Or tape the nametag to the child's clothing.

- **Ask: What is the picture on our nametags?** *(water)* **Listen to the sounds playing in our room. What do you hear?** *(water sounds)* **Water is very important in our world. Can you think of a way we use water?**

- Talk with the children about the different ways we use water, such as washing dishes, washing clothes, drinking, watering plants, bathing, and cooking.

- **Say: Water is used for something very special in the church. It is used for baptism. Our Bible story is about the time when Jesus was baptized with water.**

Water Drops

coffee filters or paper towels, scissors, food coloring, plastic containers, water, newspapers, coverups, paper punch, yarn (optional: umbrella, tape)

- Cover the work area with newspapers and have the children wear coverups.

- Partially fill plastic containers with water. Add a few drops of food coloring into each container. Make several different colors.

- Give each child a coffee filter or sheet of paper towel. Have the children cut large raindrop shapes out of the filters or towels. Encourage the children to make the raindrops as large as the papers will allow.

- Show the children how to dip the edges of their paper raindrops into the colored water. Encourage the children to watch the colors spread on the papers.

- Let each child make several raindrops. Have the children punch holes in the tops of the raindrops. Cut yarn into varying lengths. Tie the yarn through the holes and hang the raindrops from your ceiling. Or suspend an open umbrella from your ceiling. Secure the yarn and raindrops to the umbrella with tape.

- Talk with the children about the different places in nature where we find water, such as in rivers, lakes, and oceans, and from rain.

- **Say: Water is used for something very special in the church. It is used for baptism. Our Bible story is about the time when Jesus was baptized with water in a river.**

Water Works

plastic tablecloths or beach towels, tablespoons, water, buckets or cans, towels

- Create a path by spreading plastic tablecloths or beach towels on the floor end to end. Place a bucket or can partially filled with water at one end of the path. Place an empty bucket or can at the other end of the path.

- Have the children line up behind the bucket or can of water. Give the first child a tablespoon. Have the child fill the tablespoon with water and try to walk with the spoon to the other end of the path. Have the child pour the spoonful of water (or whatever water is left in the spoon) into the empty bucket or can. Then have the child tiptoe back to the line and give the spoon to the next child. Repeat the relay until every child has tried to carry a spoonful of water.

- Show the children how much water they were able to pour into the bucket or can.

- If you have a large group of children, plan for two or more lines. Let the children compare how much water each line poured into the bucket or can.

- Say: Water is important in our world. It is used for drinking and helping plants grow. Water is used to help make things clean. Water is used for something very special in the church. It is used for baptism. Our Bible story is about the time when Jesus was baptized with water in a river.

- Have the children help clean up the activities area. Encourage all the children to participate. Have towels available to dry hands and arms and to mop up spills.

Sing 'n Swing

 CD, CD player, hymnals

- Invite the children to join you in an open area of the room. Give each child a hymnal. Have the children turn to "Tell Me the Stories of Jesus." Sing the song together with the **CD.**

- Put the hymnals away. Have the children hold hands and form a circle. Choose one child to be in the middle of the circle.

- Say: *(Child's name),* **tell me about Jesus.**

- Play the song on the CD. Have the children walk around the child in the middle. Stop the music. Have the child tell something about Jesus. Help the child think of things such as, "Jesus loves me," "Jesus was born on Christmas," "Jesus is God's son," and "Jesus loves everyone."

- Then have the child choose another child to stand in the middle. Repeat the game until everyone has had an opportunity to be in the middle.

- Have the children continue to hold hands. Play and sing the song "Jesus Loves the Little Children." Break the circle and lead the children in a circle pattern into a tight circle. Then turn and unwind. Lead the children around the room as you sing. End the game in your story area.

Hand 'n Hand Bible Story

 "Jesus Is God's Son" story *(page 5)*

- Have the children sit down in your story area.

- Teach the children the hand motions for the following words. Say the words and do the motions rhythmically.

God's son. God's son.
*(Cross left hand over the right hand two times.
Cross right hand over the left hand two times.)*
Jesus is the one.
*(Pat hands on knees twice; point index finger
and move hand forward.)*
God's son. God's son.
*(Cross left hand over the right hand two times.
Cross right hand over the left hand two times.)*
Jesus is God's son.
(Pat knees twice; cross hands over chest.)

- Tell the story "Jesus Is God's Son" *(page 5).* Encourage the children to repeat the refrain and do the hand motions each time they appear in the story.

Touch the Water

 CD, CD player, sponge, Bible, bowl or dishpan, water, paper towels

- Partially fill a bowl or dishpan with water. Set the bowl or dishpan on your worship table or on the floor in front of the children.

- Choose a child to hold the Bible open to Mark 1:11.

- Say: **When Jesus was baptized, he heard God's voice. "God said, 'You are my own dear Son. I am pleased with you'" (Mark 1:11,** *Good News Bible,* **adapted).**

- Have the children repeat the verse with you. Show the children the sponge.

- Play "Water Sounds" from the **CD.** As the children listen to the sounds, toss the dry sponge to a child.

- Have the child give the sponge back to you and come to the bowl or dishpan of water. Encourage the child to dip her or his hands in the water.

- Say the Bible verse for the child. Have the child repeat the Bible verse after you.

- Give the child a paper towel to dry his or her hands. Continue the activity until every child has a turn catching the sponge, saying the Bible verse, and dipping his or her hands in the water.

Splash 'n Sing

 CD, CD player, *page 14*

- Sing the song "Drip, Drop, Splish, Splash" (*page 14*) from the **CD.** Encourage the children to sing the words to the song as they move to the music.

Drip, drop,
(*Snap fingers.*)
Splish, splash,
(*Pat knees.*)
Trickle, trickle,
(*Wiggle fingers.*)
Flow.
(*Make a sweeping motion with arms.*)

"Drip, Drop, Splish, Splash," words and music by James Ritchie;
© 1996 James Ritchie.

Baptism Booklets

 black construction paper, blue tissue or construction paper, scissors, paper punch, glue, file folders

- Have each child make a baptism booklet. The children will add to the booklet during each of the lessons on baptism.

- Give each child a piece of black construction paper. Let the children take turns using the paper punch to punch holes all over their papers. The holes will represent raindrops.

- Older children may want to cut lines to represent waves or flowing water. Show the children how to fold a two-inch strip at the bottom of their papers. Have the children use scissors to cut a wavy narrow strip off the fold. Open the fold.

- Give each child a piece of blue tissue paper or construction paper. Have the children glue their black papers on top of the blue papers. The blue water will show through the holes and cuts.

- Remind the children that water is important to our world.

- **Say: Water is used for something special in our church. Water is used for baptism. In our Bible story today Jesus was baptized with water in the Jordan River.**

- Give each child a file folder. Have the children put their water pictures inside their folders. Set the folders aside until after the trip to the sanctuary.

Visit the Baptismal Font

 Bible, Bible verse (*page 11*), **baptism certificate, baptism photos, baptismal gown, baptism booklets**

- Take the children to the sanctuary. Have the children sit on the floor near the baptismal font.

- Ask the children to recall times when they have seen people baptized in their church. Help the children remember what happens during a baptism.

- Ask the children if they remember their own baptism or the baptism of someone in their family. Let the children tell their stories.

- Share what you know about your own baptism, perhaps showing the children your, or someone else's, baptism certificate, baptismal gown, or baptism photographs.

- Read the children the story of Jesus' baptism found in Mark 1:1-11. Encourage the children to tell the story in their own words.

- **Ask: What part of the story do you think is amazing?**
  Why do you think water is used in baptism?

- Give each child a copy of the Bible verse (*page 11*). Have the children repeat the Bible verse together.

- Return to your classroom. Have the children put the copies of the Bible verse in their folders. Save the folders to use again during the next lesson.

Sing a Blessing

 CD, CD player, hymnals

- Invite the children to find "Child of Blessing, Child of Promise" in their hymnals.

- Play the song on the **CD**. Encourage the children to sing along.

- Have the children put down their hymnals and form a prayer circle.

- Ask the children to identify one thing about baptism they are thankful for.

- **Pray: Thank you, God, for the baptism of Jesus. Thank you for your love.**

- Lead the children in saying the Lord's Prayer.

Share a Salty Snack

 salty pretzels or crackers, napkins, paper cups, water, plastic pitcher

- Choose children to hand out napkins and paper cups. Serve a salty snack such as pretzels or crackers. Let the children pour water to drink from a plastic pitcher.

- Talk about how the water tastes good and refreshing after eating something salty. Remind the children that water is important in our world.

- **Pray: Thank you, God, for water to drink. Amen.**

Time to Go

 letter to parents *(page 12)*, baptism questionnaire *(page 13)*, envelopes

- Photocopy a letter to parents *(page 12)* and a baptism questionnaire *(page 13)* for each child. Place the letters and questionnaires together in envelopes.

- Have children take the questionnaires to their parents to be returned at the next lesson. Mail questionnaires to any children who were not present for today's lesson.

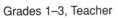

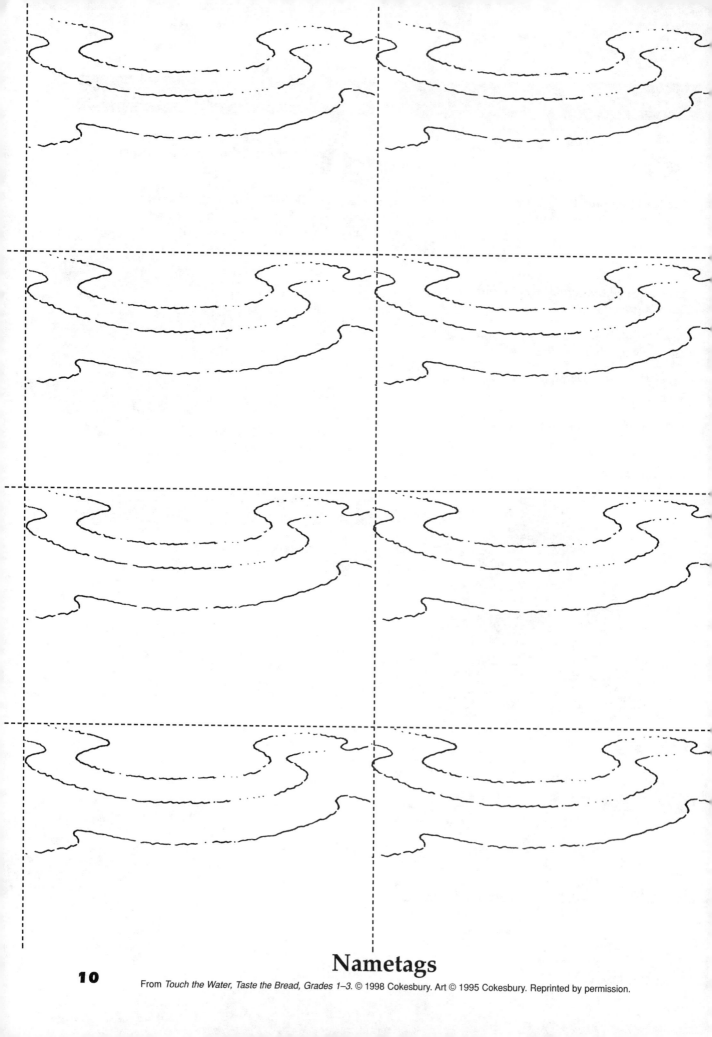

Nametags

God said, "You are my own dear Son. I am pleased with you."

Mark 1:11, Good News Bible, adapted

Bible Verse

Dear

Your child is exploring the sacrament of baptism. We need your help to make this experience meaningful to your child. Please help your daughter or son fill out the "Baptism Information" questionnaire. If your child has been baptized, the answers to the questions should be about that event. If your child has not been baptized, answer the questions for someone else in your family.

© 1994 Cokesbury.

Please have your child return this questionnaire on

_____

It will become part of a book on baptism each child is creating.

Thank you.

Letter to Parents

Baptism Information

Name of baptized person:

Date of baptism:

Place of baptism (name of church, town, country):

How old were you when you were baptized?

Who baptized you?

Who was present?

What were you wearing?

What do you or members of your family most remember about the baptism?

How did members of your family celebrate the baptism?

How has your family remembered your baptism?

Baptism Questionnaire

From *Touch the Water, Taste the Bread, Grades 1–3.* © 1998 Cokesbury. Reprinted by permission.

Drip, Drop, Splish, Splash

Drip, drop, splish, splash,
trick-le, trick-le, flow;

wa - ter, wa - ter, ev - ery - where,
love is with me ev - ery - where,
God is with me ev - ery - where,
wa - ter and the love of God,

ev - ery-where I go.

WORDS and MUSIC: James Ritchie
© 1996 James Ritchie

14

Touch the Water, Taste the Bread

Baptism

God said, "You are my own dear Son. I am pleased with you."

(Mark 1:11, *Good News Bible,* adapted)

Lesson Overview

✔ Learning Experiences	✔ Supplies	✔ Before Class
Who's Who	CD, CD player, baptism booklets, paper punch, crayons, marker, yarn or tape, scissors, nametags *(page 10)*	
Baptism Booklets	baptism booklets, file folders, dove pattern *(page 21)*, name banner *(page 22)*, scissors, tape, crayons; sandpaper, bubble wrap, or posterboard	Photocopy dove pattern and name banner.
Dove Delights	shortbread cookie dough, dove pattern *(page 17)*, thin cardboard, scissors, flour, rolling pins, cookie sheets, colored sugar or candy sprinkles, round cookie cutter or plastic cup	Prepare cookie dough.
Sing 'n Swing	CD, CD player, hymnals	
Move 'n Tell Bible Story	"The Baptism of Jesus" story *(page 16)*, baptism booklets, large piece of paper, marker	
Touch the Water	CD, CD player, sponge, Bible, bowl or dishpan, water, paper towels	
Splash 'n Sing	CD, CD player, *page 14*	
Doves in Flight	white feathers, dove puppet pattern *(page 23)*, inexpensive white paper plates, glue, scissors, craft sticks or tongue depressors, stapler, staples, crayons or markers	Photocopy dove puppet pattern.
Fly Away	CD, CD player, dove puppets	
Sing a Blessing	CD, CD player, hymnals	
Share a Snack	napkins, tray, paper cups, water, large plastic pitcher, dove delights cookies	
Time to Go	dove puppets	

The Baptism of Jesus by Charles Foster

When Jesus was a small boy, *(Stretch out arm with hand held at waist high.)*
he heard stories about a prophet who would be found in the wilderness. *(Cup hand behind ear.)*
He would be shouting, *(Cup hands around mouth.)*
"The Lord is coming!" *(Outstretch arms.)*
When Jesus was a grown man, *(Hold hand high.)*
he heard of a strange man in the wilderness, *(Cup hand behind ear.)*
baptizing people and telling them to change their ways. *(Lean down to dip hand into river; stand up and lift hand high before pouring out the water.)*
Jesus decided to go see this strange man. *(Hand over eyes as if looking into the distance.)*
So he left his village home *(Wave goodbye.)*
and walked for many miles along the road. *(Walk in place.)*
He walked over hills *(Walk in place on tiptoes.)*
and down into valleys. *(Walk in place with knees bent.)*
Eventually he left the road for a path through the grass. *(Rub hands together back and forth to make a swishing sound.)*
After many hours he reached the bank of the River Jordan. *(Pretend to walk in mud.)*
He saw many, many people listening to a man. *(Cup hands over eyes.)*
The man was called John the Baptist. *(Lean down to dip hand into river; stand up and lift hand high before pouring out the water.)*
He looked rough and wild. *(Frame face with hands.)*
His clothes were made from camel hair. *(Hold out arms as if showing off clothes.)*
People said he ate grasshoppers and honey he found in trees. *(Pretend to eat.)*
Jesus came closer *(Walk in place slowly.)*
until he could hear the man speaking. *(Cup hand behind ear.)*
"Repent!" John the Baptist shouted. "Change your ways. Be baptized so your sins will be forgiven." *(Cup hands around mouth.)*
The people crowded around him to be baptized. *(Lean down to dip hand into river; stand up and lift hand high before pouring out the water.)*
Jesus walked into the water. *(Walk in place as if moving through water.)*
John baptized Jesus. *(Lean down to dip hand into river; stand up and lift hand high before pouring out the water.)*
A dove flew down from the sky, *(Flap arms as if flying.)*
and God said, "You are my own dear Son. I am pleased with you." *(Raise hands in praise.)*

(Based on Mark 1:1-11.)

Who's Who

CD, CD player, baptism booklets, nametags (*page 10*), **crayons, marker, paper punch, scissors, yarn or tape**

- Play "Water Sounds" on the **CD** as the children arrive. Greet each child by name. Have the children put their baptism questionnaires inside their baptism booklet folders.

- If you do not know the children's names, use nametags (*page 10*) again this week. Have nametags (see page 6) available for children who were not present for the first lesson.

- As you give each child his or her nametag, **ask: What is the picture on our nametags?** (*water*) **Listen to the sounds playing in our room. What do you hear?** (*water sounds*) **Water is very important in our world. Can you think of a way we use water?**

- Remind the children about the different ways we use water, such as washing dishes, washing clothes, drinking, watering plants, bathing, and cooking.

- **Say: Water is used for something very special in the church. It is used for baptism. Our Bible story is about when Jesus was baptized with water.**

Baptism Booklets

baptism booklets, file folders, dove pattern (*page 21*), **name banner** (*page 22*), **scissors, tape, crayons, posterboard, bubble wrap, or sandpaper**

- Have each child add to the baptism booklet she or he started during the last lesson. If you have a child who did not start a booklet, give the child a file folder and let him or her begin the booklet today.

- Photocopy the dove (*page 21*) and the name banner (*page 22*) for each child. Let the children cut out the doves.

- Give each child a piece of sandpaper, posterboard, or bubble wrap. Tape the dove pattern on top of the sandpaper, posterboard, or bubble wrap. Have the children cut the doves out of the paper or wrap.

- Tape the sandpaper, posterboard, or bubble wrap dove to the table in front of each child. Lightly tape the name banner over the dove.

- Have the children use the side of a crayon with the papers removed to rub over the dove. The outline of the dove will show through the paper. If you used sandpaper or bubble wrap, the dove rubbings will show textures.

- **Say: Jesus saw a dove when he was baptized in the river. When Jesus saw the dove, he heard God's voice. "God said, 'You are my own dear Son. I am pleased with you'"** (Mark 1:11, *Good News Bible*, adapted).

- Have the children repeat the Bible verse after you.

- **Say: The dove reminds us the presence of God with us. We often call this presence the Holy Spirit. We are children of God. We know that God is always with us.**

- Have each child write her or his name in the banner space.

- **Say:** (*Child's name*) **is a child of God.**

- Give each child his or her folder. Have the children put their dove rubbings inside their folders.

- Set the folders aside to use at story time.

© 1994 Cokesbury.

Dove Delights

dove pattern *(page 17)*, thin cardboard, scissors, shortbread cookie dough, flour, rolling pins, round cookie cutter or plastic cup, cookie sheets, colored sugar or candy sprinkles

- Prepare shortbread cookie dough according to the recipe below, or buy refrigerated sugar cookie dough. Keep the cookie dough refrigerated until ready to use.

- Before class, photocopy and cut out the dove pattern *(page 17)*. Trace the dove onto thin cardboard and cut out the inside, leaving a dove stencil.

- Lightly flour the work surface. Give each child a one- to two-inch piece of cookie dough. Let the children use the rolling pin to roll their pieces of dough out flat. Place each shape on a cookie sheet.

- Let each child place the dove stencil on top of his or her cookie shape. Show the child how to sprinkle colored sugar or candy sprinkles on top of the dough. Remove the stencil. Point out the dove shape.

- **Say: Jesus saw a dove when he was baptized in the river. When Jesus saw the dove, he heard God's voice. "God said, 'You are my own dear Son. I am pleased with you'"** (Mark 1:11, *Good News Bible*, adapted).

- Have the children repeat the Bible verse.

- Bake the cookies according to the recipe while the children continue with the lesson.

Shortbread Cookies

1½ cups butter
¾ cups sugar
3 cups flour

Preheat oven to 325 degrees. Cream butter and sugar together. Gradually add flour and mix well. Give each child a one-inch piece of dough. Let the child roll the dough flat and cut it with a cookie cutter or the edge of a plastic cup. Have the child place it on an ungreased cookie sheet. Bake at 325 degrees for fifteen to twenty minutes. Makes 24 to 30 cookies.

Sing 'n Swing

CD, CD player, hymnals

- Move to an open area of the room. Give each child a hymnal. Have the children turn to "Tell Me the Stories of Jesus." Sing the song together with the **CD.**

- Put the hymnals away. Have the children hold hands and form a circle. Choose one child to be in the middle of the circle.

- **Say: (Child's name), tell me about Jesus.**

- Play the song on the CD. Have the children walk around the child in the middle. Stop the music. Have the child tell something about Jesus such as "Jesus loves me" or "Jesus was born in Bethlehem." Then have the child choose another child to stand in the middle. Repeat the game until everyone has had an opportunity to be in the middle.

- Have the children continue to hold hands. Play and sing the song "Jesus Loves the Little Children." Break the circle and lead the children in a circle pattern into a tight circle. Then turn and unwind. Lead the children around the room as you sing. End the game in your story area.

Move 'n Tell Bible Story

"The Baptism of Jesus" story *(page 16)*, baptism booklets, large piece of paper, marker

- Have the children stand in a circle with space between each child.

- **Say: Today our story is an echo pantomime. I will say a line of the story and do some motions. You are to repeat, or echo, the words and motions after me.**

- Tell the children the story "The Baptism of Jesus" *(page 16)*. If you have more than one teacher, have one teacher tell the story and another teacher do the motions.

18

- Have the children get their baptism booklets and sit down in your story area.

- Encourage each child to answer two or three questions about his or her own baptism or the baptism of some member of the family from the answers on the questionnaires.

- Help the children identify what questions they have about baptism. Write their questions on a large piece of paper. Tell the children that in the next lesson their pastor (or other person) will visit and talk about their questions.

Touch the Water

CD, CD player, sponge, Bible, bowl or dishpan, water, paper towels

- Partially fill a bowl or dishpan with water. Set the bowl or dishpan on your worship table or on the floor in front of the children.

- Choose a child to hold the Bible open to Mark 1:11.

- **Say: When Jesus was baptized, he heard God's voice. "God said, 'You are my own dear Son. I am pleased with you'" (Mark 1:11, *Good News Bible*, adapted).**

- Have the children repeat the verse with you. Show the children the sponge.

- Play "Water Sounds" from the **CD**. As the children listen to the sounds, toss the sponge to a child.

- Have the child give the sponge back to you and come to the bowl or dishpan of water. Encourage the child to dip her or his hands in the water.

- Say the Bible verse for the child. Have the child repeat the Bible verse after you.

- Give the child a paper towel to dry his or her hands. Continue the activity until every child has had a turn catching the sponge, saying the Bible verse, and dipping his or her hands in the water.

Splash 'n Sing

CD, CD player, *page 14*

- Sing together the song "Drip, Drop, Splish, Splash" *(page 14)* from the **CD**. Encourage the children to move as they sing.

> **Drip, drop,**
> (*Snap fingers.*)
> **Splish, splash,**
> (*Pat knees.*)
> **Trickle, trickle,**
> (*Wiggle fingers.*)
> **Flow.**
> (*Make a sweeping motion with arms.*)

"Drip, Drop, Splish, Splash," words and music by James Ritchie; © 1996 James Ritchie.

Doves in Flight

white feathers, dove puppet pattern (*page 23*), markers or crayons, inexpensive white paper plates, craft sticks or tongue depressors, scissors, stapler, staples, glue

- Photocopy the dove puppet pattern *(page 23)* for each child. Have the children cut out the pattern. Show the children how to trace the dove pattern onto inexpensive white paper plates. Have the children cut the doves out of the paper plates. Make one extra paper plate dove.

- Let the children decorate their doves with crayons or markers. Have the children write their names on their puppets. Have the children work together to decorate the extra dove by gluing on white feathers.

- Have each child fold his or her dove as indicated by the dotted lines on the pattern. Staple the doves onto craft sticks or tongue depressors. Complete the extra dove puppet.

- **Say: Jesus saw a dove when he was baptized in the river. When Jesus saw the dove, he heard God's voice. "God said, 'You are my own dear Son. I am pleased with you'" (Mark 1:11, *Good News Bible*, adapted).**

Fly Away

CD, CD player, dove puppets

- Invite the children to bring their dove puppets to an open area of the room. Have the children stand in a circle.

- Substitute one of the children's doves with the extra dove puppet. Help the children identify how the dove puppet is different from theirs (*it has feathers*).

- Play music from the **CD**. Have the children pass their dove puppets around the circle while the music plays.

- Stop the music. Have the child holding the feathered dove move to the middle of the circle. Encourage the child to repeat the Bible verse, "God said, 'You are my own dear Son. I am pleased with you'" (Mark 1:11, *Good News Bible*, adapted).

- Have the child return to the circle. Play the music again. Continue the game until everyone has been caught holding the feathered dove and has repeated the Bible verse.

- Have the children help clean up the paper scraps and put away the supplies. Encourage all the children to participate. Have the children set their doves aside to take home.

Sing a Blessing

CD, CD player, hymnals

- Invite the children to find "Child of Blessing, Child of Promise" in their hymnals.

- Play the song on the **CD**. Encourage the children to sing along.

- Have the children put down their hymnals and form a prayer circle.

- Ask the children to name some people who need to experience God's love.

- Pray: Thank you, God, for your love. Be with each person that we named. Amen.

- Lead the children in saying the Lord's Prayer.

Share a Snack

napkins, tray, paper cups, water, large plastic pitcher, dove delights cookies

- Pour water into a large plastic pitcher. Set paper cups on a tray. Let the children pour the drink into the cups. Remind the children that water is important in our world.

- Choose children to hand out napkins and the dove delights cookies.

- Remind the children that when Jesus was baptized, he saw a dove and heard God's voice.

- Say: The dove reminds us that the presence of God is with us. We often call this presence the Holy Spirit. We are children of God. We know that God is always with us.

- Pray: Thank you, God, for the Holy Spirit. We know you are always with us. Amen.

Time to Go

dove puppets

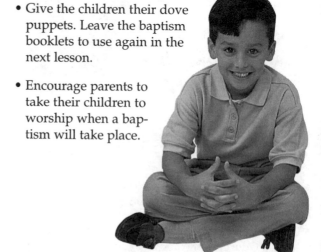

- Give the children their dove puppets. Leave the baptism booklets to use again in the next lesson.

- Encourage parents to take their children to worship when a baptism will take place.

© 1994 Cokesbury.

Dove Pattern for Name Banner

21

is a Child of God

22

Name Banner

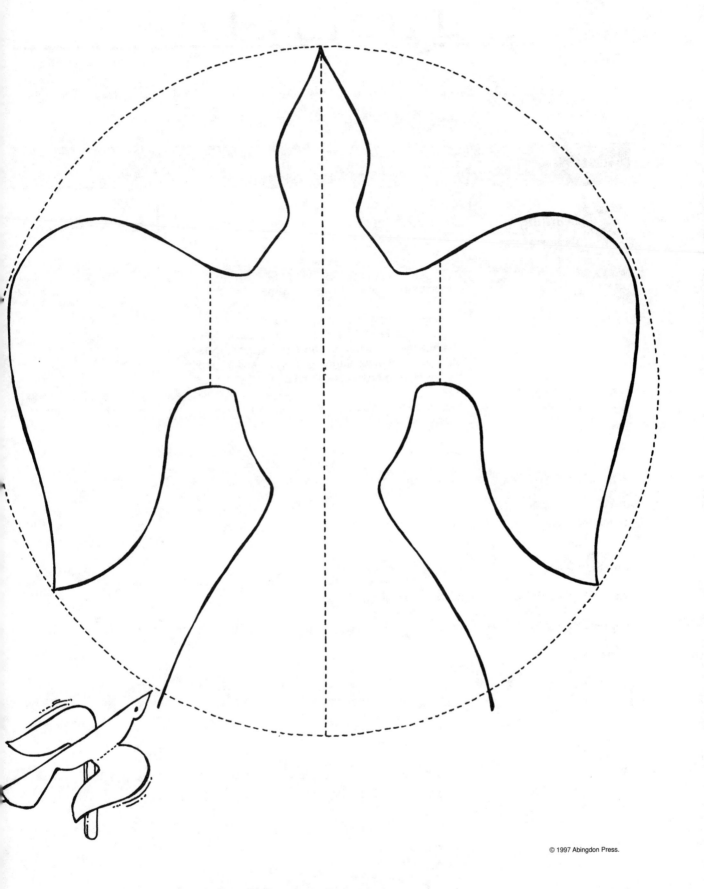

Dove Puppet Pattern

From *Touch the Water, Taste the Bread, Grades 1–3.* © 1998 Cokesbury. Reprinted by permission.

Baptism

God said, "You are my own dear Son. I am pleased with you."
(Mark 1:11, *Good News Bible*, adapted)

Lesson Overview

✓ Learning Experiences	✓ Supplies	✓ Before Class
Who's Who	CD, CD player, nametags *(page 10)*, crayons, marker, paper punch, yarn or tape, scissors	
Coverups	large piece of paper, marker; blue construction paper; white tempera paint, crayons; paper towels, shallow tray; or white construction paper, scissors, glue; handwashing supplies; large piece of paper and marker or chalkboard and chalk	
Dove Hunt	plastic dove or dove pattern (page 17), scissors, cardboard	
Sing 'n Swing	CD, CD player, hymnals	
Play 'n Tell Bible Story	"Listen and Look" play *(page 25)*, chairs or stools (optional: mural paper, markers, Bible-times costumes)	Photocopy play.
Touch the Water	CD, CD player, sponge, Bible, bowl or dishpan, water, paper towels	
Splash 'n Sing	CD, CD player, *page 14*	
Visit With Your Pastor	pastor or other guest, list of questions	
Baptism Booklets	baptism booklets, crayons or markers, plain paper	
Guess Who?	none	
God Is Pleased With Me	"God is pleased with me because" page *(page 31)*, baptism booklets and covers, pencils, stapler, staples	
Sing a Blessing	CD, CD player, hymnals	
Share a Snack	napkins, paper plates, table knives or plastic knives, ingredients for blue finger gelatin, mixing bowl, measuring cup, large spoon, 13-by-9-inch pan	Make a pan of blue finger gelatin.
Time to Go	baptism booklets	

Listen and Look by Charles Foster

Narrator: *(shout)* Listen!

Everyone: *(shout)* Listen!

Narrator: *(normal voice)* Listen, everyone.

Everyone: *(normal voice)* Listen!

Narrator: *(whisper)* Listen to the good news about Jesus.

Everyone: *(whisper)* Listen!

Narrator: *(normal voice)* Listen to the words of God from the prophet Isaiah.

Everyone: *(shout)* Listen!

Prophet: I am sending a messenger to prepare a way for you. He will be in the desert shouting, "Prepare the way for the Lord!"

Everyone: *(shout)* Listen!

Narrator: The messenger's name was John the Baptist.

Everyone: *(normal voice)* Look!

Voice 1: *(normal voice)* Look! What a strange man. His clothes must be made from camel's hair.

Voice 2: *(normal voice)* Look! He eats grasshoppers and wild honey.

Voice 3: *(whisper)* Listen! Listen to what he is saying.

Everyone: *(whisper)* Listen!

John the Baptist: *(shout)* Listen! Turn back to God and be baptized! Tell God you are sorry for the wrong things you have done.

Everyone: *(shout)* Listen!

John the Baptist: *(normal voice)* Look! Someone is coming who is more powerful than I. I baptize you with water. He will baptize you with the Holy Spirit.

Everyone: *(normal voice)* Look!

Voice 1: *(normal voice)* Look! Who is that coming?

Voice 2: *(normal voice)* Look! He comes from Nazareth.

Voice 3: *(normal voice)* Look! His name is Jesus.

Everyone: *(whisper)* Listen!

Jesus: *(normal voice)* John, I want you to baptize me.

John the Baptist: *(normal voice)* I baptize you in the name of God.

Everyone: *(whisper)* Look!

Narrator: *(whisper)* When Jesus was baptized, a dove came down to him.

Everyone: *(whisper)* Listen!

Narrator: *(whisper)* Jesus heard God's voice.

Everyone: *(whisper)* Listen!

Narrator: *(normal voice)* God said,

Everyone: *(normal voice)* "This is my own dear Son. I am pleased with him."

(Based on Mark 1:1-11.)

Who's Who

CD, CD player, nametags (*page 10*), crayons, marker, paper punch, scissors, yarn or tape

- Play "Water Sounds" on the **CD** as the children arrive. Greet each child by name.

- If you do not know the children's names, use nametags (*page 10*) again this week.

- As you give each child his or her nametag, **ask: What is the picture on our nametags?** (*water*)
Listen to the sounds playing in our room. What do you hear? (*water sounds*)
Water is very important in our world. Can you think of a way we use water?

- Remind the children about the different ways we use water, such as washing dishes, washing clothes, drinking, watering plants, bathing, and cooking.

- **Say: Water is used for something very special in the church. It is used for baptism. Our Bible story is about when Jesus was baptized with water.**

Coverups

large piece of paper, marker; blue construction paper; crayons; white tempera paint, paper towels, shallow tray; or white construction paper, scissors, glue; handwashing supplies; large piece of paper and marker or chalkboard and chalk

- Encourage the children to make covers for their baptism booklets.

- Place a folded paper towel into a shallow tray. Pour white tempera paint onto the paper towel.

- Give each child a piece of blue construction paper. Show each child how to press a hand into paint to cover the palm. Then show the child how to press the hand onto the construction paper with the fingers together and the thumb extended.

- Have the children wash their hands. Set the handprints aside to dry.

- When the handprints are dry, add a wing, feet, an eye, and a beak with crayons.

- If you choose not to use tempera paint, let the children cut handprints out of white construction paper.

- Have each child place a hand on the paper with the fingers together and the thumb extended. Trace around the hand with a crayon. The children can help each other with this activity.

- Let the children cut out their handprints.

- Give each child a piece of blue construction paper. Have the children glue their handprints onto their papers.

- Let the children use crayons to add a wing, an eye, feet, and a beak.

- **Say: Jesus saw a dove when he was baptized in the river. When Jesus saw the dove, he heard God's voice. "God said, 'You are my own dear Son. I am pleased with you'"** (Mark 1:11, *Good News Bible*, adapted).

- Write "My Book About Baptism" on a large piece of paper or on the chalkboard. Have the children copy the words onto their covers. Save the covers to use during the "God Is Pleased With Me" activity (see page 29).

- **Say: When someone is baptized, it is a special time. We are saying God loves the person being baptized. And all the people in the church are saying that they will help the person being baptized learn more about God and about Jesus. Your baptism booklets can be a keepsake about baptism.**

Dove Hunt

plastic dove or dove pattern *(page 17)*, **scissors, cardboard**

- If you cannot find a plastic dove in a crafts store, use the pattern on page 17 to cut a dove out of cardboard. Show the children the dove.

- **Say: Jesus saw a dove when he was baptized in the river. When Jesus saw the dove, he heard God's voice. "God said, 'You are my own dear Son. I am pleased with you'" (Mark 1:11, *Good News Bible*, adapted).**

- Have the children sit down in your story area. Choose a child to begin the game. Have the child step outside the classroom or close his or her eyes.

- Hide the dove somewhere in the room.

- Have the child return to the room or open her or his eyes. Have the child search the room to find the dove. When the child is close to finding the dove, have the remaining children clap their hands. When the child is moving away from the dove, have the children stomp their feet.

- When the child finds the dove, have the child bring it back to the group. Have the child hold up the dove and repeat the Bible verse.

- Let the child choose another child to look for the dove. Continue playing the game until everyone has had an opportunity to look for the dove.

- **Say: The dove reminds us that the presence of God is with us. We often call this presence the Holy Spirit. We are children of God. We know that God is always with us.**

Sing 'n Swing

CD, CD player, hymnals

- Invite the children to join you in an open area of the room. Give each child a hymnal. Have the children turn to "Tell Me the Stories of Jesus." Sing the song together with the children.

- Put the hymnals away. Have the children hold hands and form a circle. Choose one child to be in the middle of the circle.

- **Say:** *(Child's name)*, **tell me about Jesus.**

- Play the song on the CD. Have the children walk around the child in the middle. Stop the music. Have the child tell something about Jesus such as "Jesus loves children." Then have the child choose another child to stand in the middle. Repeat the game until everyone has had an opportunity to be in the middle.

- Have the children continue to hold hands. Play and sing the song "Jesus Loves the Little Children." Break the circle and lead the children in a circle pattern into a tight circle. Then turn and unwind. Lead the children around the room as you sing. End the game in your story area.

Play 'n Tell Bible Story

"Listen and Look" play *(page 25)*, **chairs or stools (optional: markers, mural paper, Bible-times costumes)**

- Photocopy the "Listen and Look" play *(page 25)* for each child.

- Assign speaking parts to the children. Choose children who are confident readers for the narrator, the prophet, John the Baptist, Jesus, and voices 1, 2, and 3. You may want to take the part of the narrator yourself. If you have less children than there are solo parts, have the children read more than one part.

- Have the children read through the play. Have all the children read the parts marked for everyone. Encourage the children to shout, speak in a normal voice, and whisper as suggested in the play.

- Set the stage for the play like a reader's theatre. Have chairs or stools placed in front of the group for the narrator, prophet, John the Baptist, and Jesus. Instruct the children reading voices 1, 2, and 3 to stand as they read.

- Have the children read through the play again.

- If you would like to expand the play into a larger project, let the children create a backdrop for the play. Mount a long piece of mural paper on the wall. Let the children draw a river scene on the mural.

- Have the children playing the narrator, the prophet, John the Baptist, and Jesus wear Bible-times costumes and stand in front of the backdrop.

Touch the Water

 CD, CD player, sponge, Bible, bowl or dishpan, water, paper towels

- Partially fill a bowl or dishpan with water. Set the bowl or dishpan on your worship table or on the floor in front of the children.

- Choose a child to hold the Bible open to Mark 1:11.

- **Say: When Jesus was baptized, he heard God's voice. "God said, 'You are my own dear Son. I am pleased with you'" (Mark 1:11, *Good News Bible*, adapted).**

- Have the children repeat the verse with you. Show the children the sponge.

- Play "Water Sounds" from the **CD.** As the children listen to the sounds, toss the sponge to a child.

- Have the child give the sponge back to you and come to the bowl or dishpan of water. Encourage the child to dip her or his hands in the water.

- Say the Bible verse for the child. Have the child repeat the Bible verse after you.

- Give the child a paper towel to dry his or her hands. Continue the activity until every child has a turn catching the sponge, saying the Bible verse, and dipping his or her hands in the water.

Splash 'n Sing

 CD, CD player, *page 14*

- Sing together the song "Drip, Drop, Splish, Splash" *(page 14)* from the **CD.** Encourage the children to move as they sing.

Drip, drop,
(*Snap fingers.*)
Splish, splash,
(*Pat knees.*)
Trickle, trickle,
(*Wiggle fingers.*)
Flow.
(*Make a sweeping motion with arms.*)

"Drip, Drop, Splish, Splash," words and music by James Ritchie;
© 1996 James Ritchie.

Visit With Your Pastor

 pastor or other guest, list of questions

- Welcome the pastor or other guest. Introduce each child to the guest. You may want to take the children back to the sanctuary and have the pastor or guest meet with the children near the baptismal font.

- Show the list of questions the children developed in the previous lesson. Let the children volunteer to read one of the questions for the pastor or guest to help answer. Encourage discussion between the pastor or guest and the children. Continue until all the questions are asked.

- Thank your guest for coming.

Baptism Booklets

 baptism booklets, crayons or markers, plain paper

- Give each child a piece of plain paper.

- **Say: Think about your own baptism or the baptism of someone in your family.**

- Let the children look at the questionnaire in their baptism booklets if they need help remembering.

- Ask: Who was present at the baptism?
  Where did the baptism take place?
  Was there a baptismal font?
  Where were the people in the congregation?
  Where was the pastor?

- Encourage the children to use the crayons or markers to draw a picture of the baptism.

- Say: When someone is baptized, it is a special time. We are saying God loves the person being baptized. And all the people in the church are saying that they will help the person being baptized learn more about God and about Jesus.

- Have the children put their completed pictures in their baptism booklets. Have the children leave their baptism booklets on the table and join you in your story area.

- Say: Jesus saw a dove when he was baptized in the river. When Jesus saw the dove, he heard God's voice. "God said, 'You are my own dear Son. I am pleased with you'" (Mark 1:11, *Good News Bible*, adapted).

- Have the children repeat the Bible verse.

- Say: God told Jesus that "I am pleased with you." This is like the joy our parents felt when we were born. They looked at us and were pleased. They loved us before we had done anything to earn that love. When we are baptized, we are reminded that God loves us before we do anything to deserve that love. God loves us because God created us.

Guess Who?

- Play an "I Spy" game with the children.

- Say: I spy someone God is pleased with. That someone has . . . (*describe one of the children in your group. You might describe what the child is wearing, what color of eyes and hair, a special talent the child has, or something the child really likes to do*).

- Continue until the group guesses who you are describing. Then let that child have a turn describing someone else. Always begin with, "I spy someone God is pleased with." Continue the game until every child has been described.

God Is Pleased With Me

"God is pleased with me because" page (*page 31*), baptism booklets and covers, pencils, staples, stapler

- Photocopy the "God is pleased with me because" page (*page 31*) for each child. Give each child a page.

- Say: When we are baptized, we are reminded that God loves us before we do anything to deserve that love. God loves us because God created us.

- Have the children think about how they would end the sentence at the top of the page.

- Say: God is pleased with me because God created me.

- Help the children think of things that make them special, things that make them somewhat different from their brothers and sisters, and things that they feel or like to do. For example, "I run fast," "I care for my little sister," "I have a good laugh," "I like to sing," or "I like to swim."

- Have the children write their statements inside the doves. Help the children fill all the doves on their pages.

- When the children finish, have the children add their pages to their baptism booklets.

- Give each child his or her dove handprint cover. Have the children stack all the pages of their baptism booklets together with the cover on top.

- Staple the left-hand side of the pages together. Set the booklets aside to send home.

Sing a Blessing

CD, CD player, hymnals

- Invite the children to find "Child of Blessing, Child of Promise" in their hymnals.

- Play the song on the **CD**. Encourage the children to sing along.

- Have the children put down their hymnals and form a prayer circle.

- Ask each child to name one way he or she knows that he or she is loved. After each child names one thing, have everyone **say: Thank you, God.**

- Lead the children in saying the Lord's Prayer.

Share a Snack

napkins, paper plates, table knives or plastic knives, ingredients for blue finger gelatin, mixing bowl, measuring cup, large spoon, 13- by 9-inch pan

- Make a pan of blue finger gelatin before class using the recipe printed above. Cut the gelatin into squares.

- Choose children to hand out napkins and paper plates. Place a square of gelatin on each child's plate.

- Give each child a table knife or a plastic knife. Let the children cut shapes out of the gelatin squares. Encourage the children to cut shapes to represent something about baptism. They might cut a water drop, wavy lines to represent water in a river, or a dove.

- Enjoy eating the finger gelatin.

Finger Gelatin

four small packages or two large
  packages of blue gelatin
2½ cups boiling water

Empty gelatin into a large mixing bowl. Pour boiling water into the bowl. Stir until the gelatin is completely dissolved. Pour the gelatin into a 13-by-9-inch pan. Place the pan in a refrigerator until the gelatin is set.

When ready to serve the finger gelatin, partially fill a sink with warm water. Dip the bottom of the pan into warm water for about fifteen seconds. Use a table knife to cut the gelatin into squares. Makes about twenty-four squares.

Time to Go

baptism booklets

- Give the children their baptism booklets to take home.

- Encourage the parents to take their children to worship when a baptism will take place.

God is pleased with me because. . .

God created me.

God Is Pleased With Me

Scriptures For Communion

Matthew 26:17-20, 26-27; Mark 14:12-17, 22-24; Luke 22:7-20

Understanding the Bible Verses

The story of Jesus' last meal with the disciples is in the Gospels of Matthew, Mark, and Luke. In Luke, Jesus breaks bread and says, "Do this in memory of me" (Luke 22:19, *Good News Bible*).

Jesus and his disciples ate the meal together in celebration of the Passover. The Passover meal reminded the Hebrews of the Israelites' escape from slavery in Egypt. The disciples had celebrated Passover all their lives, and it would have been expected for them to celebrate it in the company of Jesus this particular year.

Jesus gave the elements of the Passover meal the new interpretation that became the foundation of the Christian church's celebration of the Lord's Supper, the Eucharist, also known as Holy Communion.

Our symbols for Communion, the bread and the cup, were ordinary elements of the meal Jesus and the disciples shared. But because of Jesus' new interpretation of those items during the meal, they have become sacred symbols—reminders of Jesus' body and blood, given for us.

Understanding Your Children

Many younger elementary children have participated in Holy Communion. They have heard the words spoken by the pastor and eaten the bread and juice. The idea of "body" and "blood" being "given for you," however, are abstract concepts, and younger elementary children are not yet abstract thinkers. For them it is more important to use the celebration of Communion as a time of remembering Jesus and remembering that Jesus taught us to love and serve one another.

Younger elementary children can begin to understand that the bread and the cup are symbols of Communion. During the Last Supper Jesus shared the bread and cup with his friends and asked them to remember him. We share the bread and cup with our friends at Holy Communion and remember Jesus. As

younger elementary children grow, so will their understanding of Communion and Jesus' sacrifice for us.

Give your children tangible experiences to help that understanding. Take your children to visit the sanctuary where Communion is observed. Show them the Communion table and let them kneel at the Communion rail. Let your children touch the plate or bread basket and cup. Walk through an actual Communion service to help the children feel comfortable with the ritual and so they will know what is expected of them.

Talk to your pastor and the children's parents if you want to serve Communion as part of these lessons on Communion.

Developing Your Faith

Read Luke 22:7-20. Jesus told his disciples to remember him through the breaking of the bread and the drinking from the cup. When you think of Jesus, what is the first thing you remember? Do you remember the stories of his birth? Do you remember the stories of his death and his resurrection? Say a prayer thanking God for the gift of Jesus.

Read Mark 14:12-16. Jesus and his disciples observed the Passover meal together in the upper room of a house. This meal became the foundation

for our sacrament of Communion. Think for a moment about your own Communion experiences. What makes some memories stand out more than others? Was it the place or the people with whom you shared the sacrament?

Read Matthew 26:17-20, 26-27. We have a new relationship with God through Jesus' sacrifice. What does this new relationship mean to you? Give thanks for Jesus and his great gift to you and all people.

Communion

Do this in memory of me.
(Luke 22:19, *Good News Bible*)

Lesson Overview

✓ Learning Experiences	✓ Supplies	✓ Before Class
Who's Who	CD, CD player, nametags *(page 39)*, or markers, paper punch, scissors, yarn or tape	Photocopy and cut out nametags.
Remember Game	sponge, Communion cup, feather, paintbrush, marker, large piece of paper, plastic grapes, plastic pitcher, cup, scarf or bandanna, marker	
Sing 'n Remember	CD, CD player, *page 41*	
Move 'n Tell Bible Story	Communion cups, white felt, purple felt, "Remember Me" story *(page 34)*, symbol patterns *(page 40)*, tacks or tape, scissors	Photocopy symbol patterns.
Grape Jam Bible Verse	plastic grapes, CD, CD player, Bible	
Sing-a-Round	none	
Remember Stoles	pastor's stole, symbol patterns *(page 40)*, white felt strips, purple felt squares, scissors, white glue, lightweight posterboard or old file folders, markers	Photocopy symbol patterns. Borrow pastor's stole.
Pray 'n Remember	remember stoles	
Taste 'n Remember	crackers, grape juice, napkins, paper cups, basket	
Time to Go	none	

Remember Me by LeeDell Stickler

Sweep, sweep, sweep. (*Make sweeping motions.*) Wipe, wipe, wipe. (*Make dusting motions.*) The house must be spotlessly clean tonight. By the time everyone was finished, not a speck of dust would be left. Tonight Passover would begin.

Stir, stir, stir. (*Make stirring motions.*) Nibble, nibble, nibble. (*Pretend to taste soup with a spoon.*) Delicious smells filled the courtyard. The food had to be just right. Everything on the table tonight would have a special meaning. Even the special bread would bring to mind the story of Moses and how with God's help he led the people out of slavery in Egypt.

The sun fell behind the hills. (*Stoop down to the floor.*) The last bits of daylight faded. Everyone listened. Ooo—weee—oooo. (*Hold fists to mouth and pretend to blow a shofar.*) The sound of the shofar echoed through the streets. Everything was ready. Passover had begun.

Step, step, step. (*Pretend to walk up steps.*) Jesus' friends climbed the outside steps to the room on the roof of the house. The table was laid out. Everyone took a seat. (*Form a circle, join hands, and sit down on the floor.*) Jesus sat at the head of the table. His disciples seated themselves all around. (*Lean to the right and left pretending to talk.*) Everyone was feeling joyful. Tonight was a special night. But Jesus did not look joyful. He looked a little sad. (*Make faces look a little sad.*)

"Tonight will be the last time we will be together like this," Jesus said.

His friends looked at Jesus in surprise. (*Everyone covers mouth and makes a surprised face.*) What was Jesus talking about? Where was he going? What was going to happen?

But it was a secret for now. (*Put finger to lips.*) Jesus' friends would know soon enough.

Then Jesus took the loaf of bread from the plate. He held it up and gave thanks to God. (*Hold cupped hands as though holding a loaf of bread.*) Then he broke it into pieces and gave some to each of his friends. (*Separate hands and extend outward as though passing it to persons on right and left.*) But instead of saying the usual Passover blessings, he said, "Take this bread. From now on, whenever you eat it, I want you to remember me."

Then Jesus took the cup of wine and gave thanks to God. (*Hold hands in front of the body, forming a circle with fingers and thumbs.*) Then, instead of the usual Passover blessings, he said to his friends, "Drink from this cup. From now on, whenever you do this, remember me." (*Move hands to the right as though passing the chalice.*)

Jesus' friends were very confused. (*Put index finger to temple as though thinking.*) "What did Jesus mean, 'Remember me?' Where was he going?" (*Shrug shoulders with hands out.*) But they did not know all that was going to happen that very night.

(*Based on Luke 22:7-20.*)

Who's Who

CD, CD player, nametags *(page 39)*, crayons or markers, paper punch, scissors, yarn or tape

- Photocopy and cut out the nametags with the bread and cup pictures *(page 39)*. Make sure there is one nametag for each child.

- Play "Let Us Break Bread Together," "HA-le-lu-jah!," and "We Can Remember" on the CD as the children arrive.

- Greet each child by name. Let each child make a nametag with the bread and cup on it. Each child can print his or her name on the nametag and then color it. Use a paper punch to make a hole in the top of the nametag. Measure a length of yarn to fit easily over the child's head. Thread the yarn through the hole and tie the ends of the yarn together to make a nametag necklace. (Option: Tape the nametag to the child's clothing.)

- As the children color their nametags, **say: Your nametag has a very special picture on it. Do you recognize it? It is a cup and a loaf of bread. Can you think of a time when you have seen a cup and bread together?** *(If the children do not recall, prompt them with the following sentence.)* **Our church uses this as a very special way of remembering. It helps us remember Jesus and a special meal when Jesus shared bread and juice with his friends. At that meal, he asked his friends to remember him.**

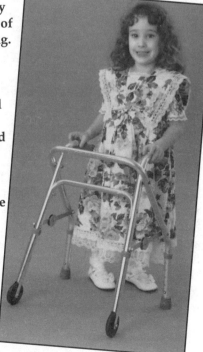

Remember Game

sponge, Communion cup, feather, paintbrush, plastic grapes, plastic pitcher, cup, scarf or bandanna, marker, large piece of paper

- Place the objects on a table. Have the children gather around the table.

- **Say: Today we are going to remember special things. Let's see how good you are at remembering. I want you to look very carefully at the items on this table. Study them very closely. I will cover them up, and we will see just how many you can remember.**

- Give the children one minute to look closely at the items. Then cover the items with the scarf or bandanna.

- **Say: Let's make a list of the items we can remember.**

- Use a marker to write the children's contributions on the large piece of paper. When the children have listed everything they can remember, remove the scarf and mark off the items that were correct.

- Option: With an older group, instead of remembering a number of objects, let the children remember the order or placement of objects. Cover the objects and let the children tell what position the objects were in. Remove the scarf or bandanna and confirm.

- **Say: Today, Jesus asks us to remember.**

Sing 'n Remember

CD, CD player, *page 41*

- Play "We Can Remember" *(page 41)* from the **CD.** Have the children form a circle in the center of the room. Add these motions to the song:

Stanza One:

You don't have to tell us or remind us a bunch.
(Shake finger to the center of the circle.)
We can remember! We can remember!
*(Hook thumbs in pretend suspenders
and puff out chest proudly.)*
You don't have to tell us,
"Please remember your lunch."
(Shake finger to the center of the circle.)
We can remember! We can remember!
(Repeat same action.)

Chorus:

We can remember!
(Hop forward.)
We can remember!
(Hop backward.)
We can remember, and it feels so good!
(Join hands and walk in a circle.)
We can remember!
(Drop hands and hop forward.)
We can remember!
(Hop backward.)
We can remember, and we knew we could!
(Turn around, then tap temple with index finger.)

Words: Stanza 1 by Nancy Ashley Young. Chorus by James Ritchie. Stanza 1 © 1994 Cokesbury. Chorus © 1990 James Ritchie.

- Repeat stanza one motions for stanzas two–five. Go over the motions several times.

- **Say: Jesus ate a special meal with his friends. As he and his friends shared the bread and the cup, Jesus asked them to remember. We can sing a song about remembering, too.**

- Play the song on the CD. Sing and move together.

- **Ask: What are some of the things the song talks about remembering?** *(Not to forget lunch, homework, feed the pet, what parents tell us to do, when to get up, turn out the light.)*
What is it in the song that Jesus asks us to remember? *(Remember Jesus when we eat the bread or drink the cup.)*

Move 'n Tell Bible Story

Communion cups, white felt, purple felt, "Remember Me" story *(page 34)*, symbol patterns *(page 40)*, tacks or tape, scissors

- Photocopy the bread and cup from the symbol patterns *(page 40)*. Use the patterns to cut the bread and cup out of the purple felt.

- Place the white felt across your worship table or mount the felt on a bulletin board or wall in your storytelling area.

- Bring the children together in the storytelling area. Make sure there is room for them to move about freely.

- **Say: I want you to help me tell the story. As I tell the story, I will do certain actions. I want you to do just what I do. Our Bible story tells about a time when Jesus shared a special meal with his friends. This meal was the Passover meal. Passover was a special holiday. During this time the people remembered how Moses with God's help had led the Hebrew people out of slavery in Egypt. Every year the people came together in Jerusalem to celebrate. They had special foods and did special things that would help them remember.**

- Tell the story "Remember Me" *(page 34)* and do the motions.

- **Ask: What did Jesus ask his friends to do?** *(remember him)*
What would help them remember? *(the bread and the cup)*

- Place the purple felt bread and cup on the white felt.

- **Say: We remember Jesus too. We have a special meal at church to remember Jesus. We call the special meal Communion. We use the cups of juice** *(Give each child a Communion cup to hold.)* **and small pieces of bread. These remind us of the special meal Jesus shared with his friends. When we do this, we remember Jesus. We remember Jesus loves us. We remember that Jesus is always with us.**

Grape Jam Bible Verse

plastic grapes, CD, CD player, Bible

- Have the children form a circle on the floor.

- Say: Jesus told us to remember him whenever we ate the bread and drank from the cup. In fact, our Bible verse for today tells us this.

- Open the Bible to Luke 22:19 and read the verse.

- Ask: Can you say this with me? (*Have the children repeat it with you.*)
  Can you say it very loudly? (*Have the children say it loudly.*)
  Can you say it very softly? (*Have the children say it softly.*)
  Can you say it very wavy? (*Have the children say it wavy.*)

- Hold up the bunch of plastic grapes.

- Say: I am going to start the grapes around the circle as the music plays. When the music stops, whoever has the grapes will stand up, say the Bible verse, come to the center of the circle, and sit down.

- Begin the music on the CD. Stop and start it frequently so that soon everyone in the group is in the center of the circle.

- Say: Now, think like a bunch of grapes that has been squished into jam. I want you to hold onto the person next to you and everyone try to stand up together.

Sing-a-Round

- Have the children stand in a circle, holding hands. Sing the song "Jesus Blessed and Broke the Bread" to the tune of "London Bridge Is Falling Down."

- Sing the first stanza walking to the right. Sing the second stanza walking to the left. Sing the final stanza stepping into and out of the circle. Repeat the song several times.

Jesus blessed and broke the bread,
Broke the bread, broke the bread;
Jesus blessed and broke the bread
After supper.

Jesus blessed and passed the cup,
Passed the cup, passed the cup;
Jesus blessed and passed the cup,
After supper.

When we take the bread and cup,
Bread and cup, bread and cup;
When we take the bread and cup,
We remember.

Words: Jim Ritchie.
© 1988 Graded Press. Revised © 1991, 1995 Cokesbury.

- Say: Jesus shared the bread and cup with his friends. He asked his friends to remember him. When we remember Jesus, we remember that he taught us to love and serve others.

Remember Stoles

pastor's stole; symbol patterns (*page 40*); white felt strips (four inches wide by 48 inches long), one for each child; purple felt squares, four for each child; scissors; white glue, lightweight posterboard or old file folders; marker

- Photocopy the symbol patterns (*page 40*). Cut out the patterns and trace them onto lightweight posterboard or old file folders. Provide several of each pattern.

- Make arrangements to borrow one of your pastor's stoles, preferably the one he or she wears for Communion.

- Say: When we remember Jesus, we remember all that Jesus taught. Jesus taught us to love one another.

- Ask: What other things do you remember about Jesus? (*Allow the children to share stories they remember.*)

- Hold up the stole that you borrowed from your pastor.

- Ask: Where have you seen a stole such as this? (*The pastor wears one on Sunday morning.*) When the pastor wears this stole, it becomes a symbol of serving others. Jesus taught us to love and serve others. We can make a stole to wear on our final lesson to show that as Christians, we can serve others just as Jesus taught.

- Give each child a white felt stole and four squares of purple felt.

- Talk about the symbols with the children. Help the children remember what each symbol represents: cup and bread–Communion; heart–love; dove–Holy Spirit.

- Let the children choose patterns that remind them of Jesus. Or they may cut their own design. Have the children use a marker to trace around the patterns on the purple felt.

- Have the children cut out the shapes and glue them onto the stoles. Make sure the shapes are at least three inches from either end. Children may choose to fringe the ends of their stoles by cutting narrow strips.

- **Say: The stoles remind us that Jesus taught us to love and serve others. When we follow Jesus' example, we are remembering Jesus.**

- Have the children clean up the area.

Pray 'n Remember

 remember stoles

- Invite the children to bring their stoles and stand in a circle.

- Have the children hold their stoles in front of them.

- Go to each child in the circle, take the stole, and place it over the child's shoulders.

- **Say: (Child's name), remember that Jesus loves you.**

- After everyone is wearing her or his stole, pray the Lord's Prayer together.

- Collect the stoles to use in the third lesson on Communion. Let the children know that they will use their stoles when you celebrate Communion together.

Taste 'n Remember

 crackers, grape juice, napkins, paper cups, basket

- Place the crackers in a basket. Pour grape juice into cups before class. Select children to hand out napkins and to pass the basket around the group. Give each child a cup of juice.

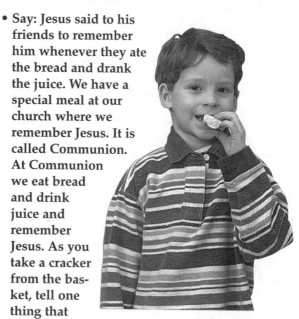

- **Say: Jesus said to his friends to remember him whenever they ate the bread and drank the juice. We have a special meal at our church where we remember Jesus. It is called Communion. At Communion we eat bread and drink juice and remember Jesus. As you take a cracker from the basket, tell one thing that you remember about Jesus. After each statement, everyone will say "We remember Jesus."**

- When everyone has a cracker, **pray: Dear God, we thank you for Jesus. Help us to remember Jesus as we love and serve others. Amen.**

Time to Go

 none

- Remind the children you will save their stoles to use when you celebrate Communion.

- Make arrangements with your pastor to serve Communion to the children (see page 57). Let parents know when you plan to celebrate Communion with the children.

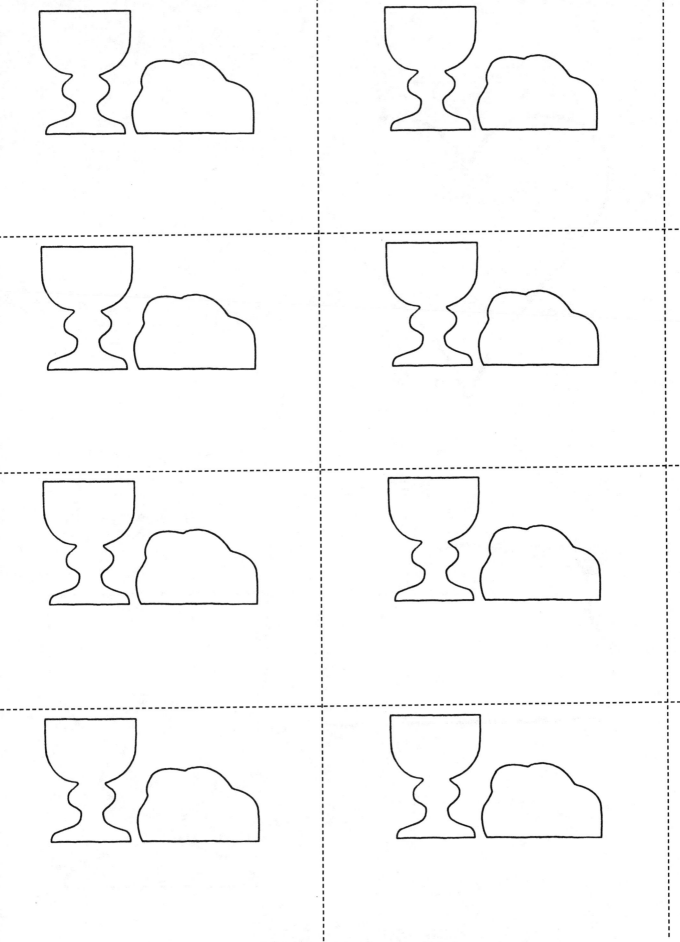

Nametags

39

Symbol Patterns

We Can Remember

WORDS: Stanzas 1-4 by Nancy Ashley Young. Stanza 5 by James Ritchie.
MUSIC: James Ritchie; arr. by Timothy Edmonds
Words and music © 1990 James Ritchie. Stanzas 1-4 © 1994 Cokesbury.

Communion

Do this in memory of me.

(Luke 22:19, *Good News Bible*)

Lesson Overview

✓ Learning Experiences	✓ Supplies	✓ Before Class
Who's Who	CD, CD player, nametags *(page 39)*, crayons or markers, paper punch, scissors, yarn or tape	
Worship Hands	see page 44	
Worship Chalices	see page 45	
Worship Cloth	see page 45	
Sing 'n Swing	CD, CD player, crepe paper, *page 51*, masking tape, scissors	
Sign 'n Tell Bible Story	"We Remember" story *(page 43)*	
Visit the Sanctuary	Communion items, pastor or Communion steward	Make arrangements with pastor or Communion steward to meet with children.
Bible Verse Jumble	CD, CD player, Bible verse jumble *(page 49)*, drinking straws, masking tape, scissors	Photocopy page 49.
Sing-a-Round	none	
Great Grapes	plastic grapes, Communion cups, Bible verse *(page 50)*, blue, purple, and green tempera paint, cotton swabs, newspaper, coverups, cleanup supplies, shallow trays, paper towels	Photocopy page 50.
Pray 'n Remember	*page 43*	
Taste the Grapes	white and purple seedless grapes, napkins, paper cups, grape juice or water	
Time to Go	Bible verse posters	

We Remember by LeeDell Stickler

Tiny baby in a manger,
God's son sleeping on the hay.
Shepherds heard the angel chorus.
Wise men came from far away.

We remember Jesus.

Jesus grew to be a teacher,
Called disciples, "Follow me."
Fisherman Peter and his brother,
Ordinary folks like you and me.

We remember Jesus.

Jesus showed us how to love.
Jesus showed us how to care.
Jesus showed us God's forgiveness.
Jesus taught us all to share.

We remember Jesus.

Jesus welcomed little children,
"Let the children come to me."
Jesus healed the sick and hopeless,
Wanting all God's love to see.

We remember Jesus.

Jesus rode into the city
On a tiny donkey gray.
People greeted him with branches,
Laid their cloaks down in his way.

We remember Jesus.

In a cozy upper room
That evening when the sun went down,
Jesus and his loyal friends
Joyfully did gather round.

We remember Jesus.

Jesus took the bread and broke it,
Gave it to his friends to share.
Jesus took the cup and blessed it,
Passed it to those who gathered there.

We remember Jesus.

Jesus smiled at all his friends,
"When you take this cup and bread,
I want you to remember
All I've done and all I've said."

We remember Jesus.

In our church we still remember
All that Jesus did and said,
As we gather at the altar,
Drink the juice, and eat the bread.

We remember Jesus.

"I will always be there,"
Jesus told his friends.
And that is just as true today;
His love will never end.

We remember Jesus.

Who's Who

 CD, CD player, nametags *(page 39)*, crayons or markers, paper punch, scissors, yarn or tape

- Greet the children as they arrive. Play "Let Us Break Bread Together," "HA-le-lu-jah," and "We Can Remember" on the **CD** as the children come into the room and while they are working. Greet each child by name. If you do not know the children's names, use the nametags *(page 39)* again this week. Have nametags (see page 35) available for children who were not present for the first lesson.

- As you give each child his or her nametag, **say: The picture on the nametag shows a loaf of bread and a cup. This picture reminds me of a special story about Jesus and his friends. They ate a special meal together. At the end of the meal Jesus shared the bread and the cup with his friends and asked them to remember all that he had taught them.**

- Invite the children to share their favorite stories about Jesus.

- Invite the children to prepare a worship center for Communion by making a banner, chalices, and a cloth (see the following activities).

- **Say: In our last lesson we made special worship stoles. We will wear these stoles on our last lesson. Each stole has pictures on it that remind us of Jesus. Today we are going to decorate our worship area in a special way. We will make a special cross of handprints; we will make a special worship cloth; and we will make the chalices we will use during the worship time.**

- Encourage the children to do all the activities, but allow them to choose which one they want to do first.

Worship Hands

 white burlap (three feet wide by five feet long), purple felt squares, scissors, pencils, felt-tip markers, glitter, scraps of colored felt, fabric paints, glue (optional: purple construction paper, colored construction paper)

- Lightly draw the outline of a cross with a felt-tip marker on a piece of white burlap. The cross pieces should be slightly wider than a handprint. Place the cross outline on a table so that it is easily accessible for the children.

- **Say: Purple is a special color to the church. We use it at special times of the year. In the time called Lent, which is just before Easter, we use purple. In the time of Advent, the time just before Christmas Day, we use purple.**

- Have the children trace around their hands on the purple felt. Some children may want to work in pairs and have one child trace the hand of the other child. Cut out the hands and let each child decorate the handprint with scraps of colored felt, fabric paints, or glitter. (Optional: Use purple construction paper and scraps of colored construction paper, glitter, and markers.)

- When each child finishes his or her handprint, glue the handprint within the outline of the cross.

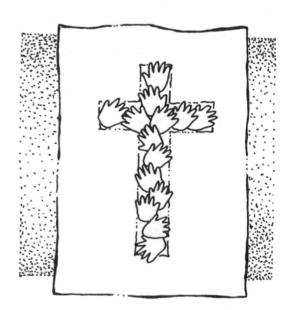

Worship Chalices

 clear plastic cups (two sizes, one smaller than the other), masking tape, purple ribbon (one inch wide), scissors, white glue, newspaper (optional: sequins, jewels, braid)

- Cover the work surface with newspapers. Each child will need: two clear plastic cups (one larger, one smaller), masking tape, purple ribbon, and white glue.

- Place the smaller cup upside down on a table. Place the larger cup right side up on top of the smaller cup, matching the bases. Run a strip of masking tape around the two bases, joining them together into one form.

- Cut a strip of purple ribbon long enough to go around the two bases. Lay the ribbon on the newspaper, shiny side down. Put glue on the ribbon, making sure the entire side of the ribbon is covered.

- Place the ribbon over the masking tape. (Option: Sequins, jewels, and braid will add elegance to the chalice.)

- Children will use these chalices for the grape juice during the Communion service. Avoid placing any decorations around the lip of the cup.

Worship Cloth

 large piece of white cloth (sheeting works well); felt-tip markers; newspaper; coverups; old curriculum, Bible storybooks, children's Bibles (optional: drawing paper)

- Spread the newspaper on the floor. Put the white cloth over the newspaper. Have the children wear coverups.

- Say: When Jesus had his special meal with his friends, he asked them to remember him and all that he had taught them. I want you to think of your favorite story about Jesus. We will draw the stories onto our worship cloth so that next week we will have a collection of stories about Jesus. *(You may want the children to sketch out their design on drawing paper before they draw it on the worship cloth.)*

- Encourage the children to choose different stories. Look through old curriculum, Bible storybooks, children's Bibles, and so forth for ideas.

Sing 'n Swing

 CD, CD player, crepe paper, *page 51*, masking tape, scissors

- Cut the **crepe paper** into four-foot lengths. Put two together, fold them in half, and tape the end with masking tape to form a small handle. Give each child a set of the streamers.

- Say: Jesus invited his friends to share a special meal with him. During this meal he asked his friends to remember him whenever they ate the bread and drank from the cup. Today in church during Holy Communion we remember Jesus. We remember what Jesus taught and did. Communion is a special time when the whole church comes together to celebrate as the family of God.

- Play the song "HA-le-lu-jah!" *(page 51)* from the **CD.** Invite the children to move to the music and to use their streamers as they sing.

- Suggestion: Raise streamers overhead and punch upward on "HA." Then bring the streamers down and shake lightly in front of the body.

Sign 'n Tell Bible Story

"We Remember" story *(page 43)*

- Bring the children together into the storytelling area. They may sit on the floor or in chairs.

- **Say: Today we are going to remember Jesus, just as he told us to do that night when he ate the special meal with his friends. As you listen to the story, you will hear some stories you may remember. At the end I will ask you to list the stories you heard. As we tell the story, I want you to help. Every time I say, "We remember Jesus," I want you to sign the words and say the words with me.**

- Teach the children the signs for "We remember Jesus." The signs are pictured with the story on page 43. Practice with the children several times.

- Tell the story "We Remember" *(page 43)* using the signs.

Visit the Sanctuary

Communion items, pastor or Communion steward

- Take the children to the sanctuary to see where the people in your church celebrate Communion. Ask your pastor or Communion steward to set out the items your church uses for Communion.

- **Say: Our church has a special time to remember Jesus. It is called Communion. At Communion we eat the bread and drink the juice and remember Jesus.**

- Invite the pastor or Communion steward to meet the children and let the children walk through the motions of how your church serves Communion. Let the children kneel at the altar rail if this is appropriate for your church. Show the children how the elements are passed. Talk about the form that is used in your congregation.

Bible Verse Jumble

CD, CD player, Bible verse jumble *(page 49)*, drinking straws, masking tape, scissors

- Make a copy of the Bible verse jumble *(page 49)*. If you have eighteen children, cut each letter apart. Use masking tape to attach each letter to a plastic drinking straw. If you have fewer than eighteen children, cut two consecutive letters together to make one card with two letters. Tape the pairs of letters to drinking straws. Mix up the letter straws and give them to the children.

- **Say: Let's repeat the Bible verse together: "Do this in memory of me" (Luke 22:19,** *Good News Bible***). Let's say it again very slowly.** *(Repeat the verse, dragging it out.)* **Let's say it again very quickly.** *(Repeat the verse quickly.)*

- **Say: The letters you are holding when put in the correct order will make the words of our Bible verse. I am going to play a song. As we play the music, you will pass the letters to the right. When the music stops, everyone has to get in the order of the words to spell the Bible verse.**

- Play "We Can Remember" from the **CD.** Stop the music and let the children get themselves in order of the words. Scramble the letters again and repeat the game as the children show interest.

Sing-a-Round

 none

- Have the children stand in a circle, holding hands. Sing the song "Jesus Blessed and Broke the Bread" to the tune of "London Bridge Is Falling Down."

- Sing the first stanza walking to the right. Sing the second stanza walking to the left. Sing the final stanza stepping into and out of the circle. Repeat the song several times.

> **Jesus blessed and broke the bread,**
> **Broke the bread, broke the bread;**
> **Jesus blessed and broke the bread**
> **After supper.**
>
> **Jesus blessed and passed the cup,**
> **Passed the cup, passed the cup;**
> **Jesus blessed and passed the cup**
> **After supper.**
>
> **When we take the bread and cup,**
> **Bread and cup, bread and cup;**
> **When we take the bread and cup,**
> **We remember.**

Words: Jim Ritchie.
© 1988 Graded Press. Revised © 1991, 1995 Cokesbury.

- **Say: Jesus shared the bread and cup with his friends. He asked his friends to remember him. When we remember Jesus, we remember that he taught us to love and serve others.**

Great Grapes

 plastic grapes; Communion cups; Bible verse *(page 50)*; blue, purple, and green tempera paint; cotton swabs; newspaper; coverups; cleanup supplies; shallow trays; paper towels

- Invite the children to make a special Bible verse poster to take home. Each child will need two plastic Communion cups.

- Photocopy the Bible verse *(page 50)* for each child. Read the Bible verse together.

- Show the children the plastic grapes.

- **Ask: Where does grape juice come from?** *(It comes from grapes.)*
  Where does bread come from? *(It comes from flour, which comes from grain.)*

- **Say: During the special meal Jesus shared with his friends, he told them to remember him every time they ate the bread or drank the cup. Today, all people are invited to remember Jesus. During Communion the pastor invites us to come to the table and eat the bread and drink the juice. When we do this, we are remembering Jesus.**

- Cover the tables with newspaper. Have the children wear coverups. Place a paper towel in the bottom of a shallow tray to make a paint pad. Pour a small amount of purple paint onto the paper towel. Make a second paint pad with the blue paint.

- Dip the rims of the Communion cups into the paint and then press them evenly onto the Bible verse poster. Overlap the circles to create a bunch of grapes. Use one cup in the purple and one in the blue. Older children may want to use cotton swabs to smear a little paint on the curved edge of each grape, giving the grapes a three-dimensional look.

- When the children have completed the bunch of grapes, let them create the grape leaves. Make a paint pad of green paint in a third shallow tray. Let the children dip their flattened hand into the paint and then onto the paper to make the grape leaves. Have cleaning supplies within close reach.

- Set the pictures aside to dry.

Taste the Grapes

 white and purple seedless grapes, napkins, paper cups, grape juice or water

- Select children to hand out napkins and paper cups. Pour grape juice or water into the cups.

- Let the children sample the different kinds of grapes. Have them chew each kind slowly, savoring the taste and the juice.

- Say: **Close your eyes as you taste each grape. Try to tell the difference between the white grape and the purple grape. We buy our grape juice from the store. Imagine how the people in Jesus' time got their grape juice.**

- Pray: **Thank you, God, for grapes and grape juice. Help us to remember Jesus. Amen.**

Time to Go

 Bible verse posters

- Give the children their Bible verse posters.

- Collect the nametags for Lesson 3. Place them on the door or in a special area where the children can get them as they arrive next week.

Pray 'n Remember

 page 43

- Have the children sit down in your story area.

- Sign "We remember Jesus" (see page 43). Then choose a child from your group.

- Say: *(Child's name)* **is a special child of God.**

- Have that person stand up and sign, "We remember Jesus." Call on each child until everyone is standing up. Have the children join hands.

- Pray: **Dear God, we thank you for Jesus. Help us to remember all he taught and to follow his example.**

- Pray the Lord's Prayer together.

Bible Verse Jumble

Do this in memory of me.

(Luke 22:19, Good News Bible)

Bible Verse

HA-le-lu-jah!

WORDS and MUSIC: James Ritchie

Grades 1–3, Teacher

Communion

Do this in memory of me.

(Luke 22:19, *Good News Bible*)

Lesson Overview

✓ Learning Experiences	✓ Supplies	✓ Before Class
Who's Who	CD, CD player, nametags *(page 39)*	
Bread Baskets	lunch-size paper bags, construction paper, white glue or tape, scissors	Cut colored construction paper into 1-by-14-inch strips
Sing 'n Swing	CD, CD player, *page 51,* crepe paper	
Say 'n Tell Bible Story	"We Remember" story *(page 53)*, word cards *(pages 58 and 59)*, scissors	Photocopy word cards.
Galloping Grapes	plastic grapes, Bible	
Experience Bread	Bible, meat hammer, cutting board, barley, newspaper	
Communion Bread	ingredients for bread, cooking utensils	
Taste the Bread	different kinds of bread (tortilla, bagel, matzo, cornbread, pita bread, French baguette), paper plates, napkins, bread baskets, cups, water or juice (optional: honey, butter, or jam)	
Sing-a-Round	none	
Get Ready to Worship	see page 57	
Celebrate Communion	see page 57	
Pray 'n Go	grocery-size paper bags, stoles, bread baskets, chalices, marker	

We Remember   by LeeDell Stickler

Tiny baby in a **manger**,
God's son sleeping on the **hay**.
Shepherds heard the **angel** chorus.
Wise men came from far away.

We remember Jesus.

Jesus grew to be a **teacher**,
Called disciples, "Follow me."
Fisherman Peter and his **brother**,
Ordinary folks like you and me.

We remember Jesus.

Jesus showed us how to **love**.
Jesus showed us how to care.
Jesus showed us God's forgiveness.
Jesus taught us all to **share**.

We remember Jesus.

Jesus welcomed little **children**,
"Let the children come to me."
Jesus healed the **sick** and hopeless,
Wanting all God's love to see.

We remember Jesus.

Jesus rode into the city
On a tiny donkey gray.
People greeted him with **branches**,
Laid their cloaks down in his way.

We remember Jesus.

In a cozy upper **room**,
That evening when the sun went
   down,
Jesus and his loyal **friends**
Joyfully did gather round.

We remember Jesus.

Jesus took the **bread** and broke it,
Gave it to his friends to share.
Jesus took the **cup** and blessed it,
Passed it to those who gathered
   there.

We remember Jesus.

Jesus smiled at all his friends,
"When you take this **cup** and **bread,**
I want you to remember
All I've done and all I've said."

We remember Jesus.

In our church we still remember
All that Jesus did and said,
As we gather at the **altar,**
Drink the juice, and eat the **bread.**

We remember Jesus.

"I will always be there,"
Jesus told his friends.
And that is just as **true** today;
His **love** will never end.

We remember Jesus.

Who's Who

CD, CD player, nametags *(page 39)*

- Play "Let Us Break Bread Together," "HA-le-lu-jah!," and "We Can Remember" on the **CD** as the children arrive today.

- Greet each child with: **Welcome, *(child's name)*. You are a child of God.**

- As you give each child his or her nametag (see page 39), **say: The picture on the nametag shows a loaf of bread and a cup. This picture reminds me of a special meal Jesus ate with his friends. At the end of the meal Jesus shared the bread and the cup with his friends and asked them to remember all that he had taught them. In church we remember Jesus at a special meal called Communion.**

Bread Baskets

one lunch-size paper bag for each child, construction paper (11-by-14- inch strips), white glue or tape, scissors

- Have each child make a bread basket to use for the different varieties of bread later in the lesson.

- **Say: We remember that Jesus ate a special meal with his friends. Our church has a special meal to remember Jesus. It is called Communion. At Communion we eat bread and drink juice and remember Jesus. Let's make bread baskets to hold different kinds of bread.**

- Prior to class cut the colored construction paper into 1-by-14-inch strips. Set the strips out on a table so the children can choose the colors they want.

- Have the children open their lunch bags and set them on the table.

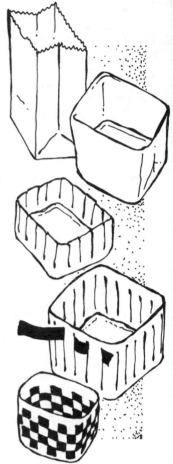

- Fold the top edge of the bag to the inside until it touches the bottom of the bag. Fold in half to the inside again.

- Make cuts through the fold about one inch apart. Leave approximately one inch around the base of the sack uncut. Unfold the second fold.

- Each child may choose two or three strips of construction paper with which to weave his or her basket. Show the children how to weave the strip over and under each cut in the paper bag. Remind them if the first strip begins over the flap, the second strip should begin under. Glue or tape the ends together when you have made one complete round. Then begin another strip.

Sing 'n Swing

CD, CD player, crepe paper, *page 51*

- Have the children stand in a circle.

- Give each child the blue crepe paper streamers.

- **Say: Jesus invited his friends to share a special meal with him. During this meal he also asked his friends to remember him whenever they ate the bread and drank from the cup. Today in church during Holy Communion we remember Jesus. We remember all that Jesus taught and did. Communion is a special time when the whole church comes together to celebrate as the family of God.**

- Play the song "HA-le-lu-jah!" *(page 51)* from the **CD.** Sing the song together. Invite the children to move to the music and to use their streamers.

- Suggestion: Raise streamers overhead and punch upward on "HA." Then bring the streamers down and shake lightly in front of the body.

Say 'n Tell Bible Story

"We Remember" story *(page 53)*, word cards *(pages 58 and 59)*, scissors

- Photocopy the word cards *(pages 58 and 59)*. Cut apart the words. Give one word to each child. Have the children say their words out loud.

- **Say: You are going to help me tell the story. A word thief sneaked into the story we used last week and cut some of the words out. As I read, I will come to a place where a word is missing. If you think it is your word, stand up and shout it out.**

- Read the story, "We Remember" *(page 53)*, pausing at the words in boldface type.

- If you have a small group of children, give each child more than one word. If you have a large group of children, tell the story more than once and let the children take turns saying the words.

Galloping Grapes

plastic grapes, Bible

- Have the children sit in a circle. Choose one child to read the Bible verse, "Do this in memory of me" (Luke 22:19, *Good News Bible*). Have all the children repeat the Bible verse. Show the children the plastic grapes.

- **Say: Let's play a game to help us learn the Bible verse. You will pass the grapes around the circle. The first person will pass the grapes and say the first word of the Bible verse. The second person will pass the grapes and say the second word of the Bible verse. The third person will pass the grapes and say the third word and so on. Let's see how fast the verse can travel.**

- Practice saying the verse very slowly. Then say: "Go!" and start the game. Go around the circle several times. Have the children speed up every time you say, "faster!"

- When the children know the verse well, let them pass the grapes back and forth across the circle.

Experience Bread

Bible, meat hammer, cutting board, barley, newspaper

- **Say: Bread is something people at all times and in all places eat. In Bible times the ordinary food of the average family was bread, olives, oil, buttermilk, cheese, fruits and vegetables from their orchards and gardens, and meat on rare occasions. The main food, however, was bread. In fact, the word *bread* was often used to mean all the food that a person needed to eat. If a family was seated "breaking bread," they would not rise to greet a guest until they were finished. This showed the importance of bread. Everything about bread, from the sowing of the seed to the baking of the loaves, was done in the name of God.**

- Read the following Scripture references to the children: Matthew 6:11, John 6:35.

- **Say: Because bread was regarded so highly, the custom of breaking bread came into being. A knife was never used to cut bread. Bible times people always broke it into pieces with their fingers.**

- **Say: When we want bread, we go to the grocery store. But in Bible times people had to make their own bread. Not only did they make their own bread, they made the flour that made the bread. The poorer families had bread made of barley. When Jesus fed the 5,000 people, the boy who gave his loaves to Jesus had barley loaves. A family who was well-to-do had bread made from wheat flour.**

- Give the children the opportunity to grind barley into flour. Cover the floor with newspaper. Place a few barley grains on a wooden or Lucite cutting board. Let the children pound the barley until it forms flour. Make sure the children keep their fingers and hands from beneath the meat hammer.

Communion Bread

ingredients for bread, cooking utensils

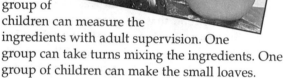

- Let the children bake bread to use for Communion. Use the recipe printed below.

- Depending on the number of children you have, set up stations for making bread. One group of children can measure the ingredients with adult supervision. One group can take turns mixing the ingredients. One group of children can make the small loaves.

Communion Bread

¾ cup butter
¾ cup sugar
¼ teaspoon salt
1 cup sour milk or add 1 tablespoon vinegar to 1 cup milk
¼ teaspoon baking soda
1 teaspoon baking powder
4 cups all-purpose flour
flour for kneading

Preheat oven to 350 degrees. Cream butter and sugar together. Add remaining ingredients in the order listed. Mix well. Give each child a golf ball-size piece of dough. Let the children shape the dough into flat loaves on a floured surface. Place each loaf on a baking sheet. Bake at 350 degrees for ten to fifteen minutes. Let cool before eating. Makes 24 to 28 small loaves.

Taste the Bread

different kinds of breads (tortilla, bagel, matzo, cornbread, pita bread, French baguette, and so forth), paper plates, napkins, bread baskets, cups, water or juice (optional: honey, butter, or jam)

- Place the different varieties of bread into the baskets the children made.

- **Say: Bread is eaten all over the world. But bread doesn't always look the same. Bread is not always made from the same kinds of grain.**

- Select children to hand out paper plates, napkins, and cups of water or juice. Have the children go around the table and taste the different kinds of bread. (Optional: Provide honey, butter, or jam.)

- When the children have had the opportunity to taste the different varieties, **ask: What was your favorite kind of bread? What was your least favorite kind of bread? What bread looked different from bread that you are familiar with? Was there any bread that surprised you? Was there any kind of bread that you had never tasted before?**

Sing-a-Round

- Have the children stand in a circle, holding hands. Sing the song "Jesus Blessed and Broke the Bread" to the tune of "London Bridge Is Falling Down."

- Sing the first stanza walking to the right. Sing the second stanza walking to the left. Sing the final stanza stepping into and out of the circle. Repeat the song several times.

> **Jesus blessed and broke the bread,**
> **Broke the bread, broke the bread;**
> **Jesus blessed and broke the bread**
> **After supper.**

Jesus blessed and passed the cup,
Passed the cup, passed the cup;
Jesus blessed and passed the cup,
After supper.

When we take the bread and cup,
Bread and cup, bread and cup;
When we take the bread and cup,
We remember.

Words: Jim Ritchie.
© 1988 Graded Press. Revised © 1991, 1995 Cokesbury.

Get Ready to Worship

stoles (*Lesson 1*); chalices, worship cloth, handprint cross (*Lesson 2*); bread (*Lesson 3*); basket, pitcher of grape juice, candles, matches, Bible

- Prepare the worship center for Communion. If the pastor is unable to officiate the service, then instead of Communion, have a love feast.

- Place the cross made from the children's handprints behind the worship center. Cover the table with the worship cloth the children made in Lesson 2. Place the open Bible on the worship center. Place a candle on the worship center and light it to symbolize the presence of God. Always keep matches out of the children's reach.

- Let one or more children put the warm bread in a basket and place it on the worship center. Pour a small amount of juice into each chalice.

Celebrate Communion

items listed in "Get Ready to Worship" (optional: platters, cheese, grapes, dates, olives, figs or fig cookies, pomegranate)

- Have the children put on their stoles and get their chalices.

- Say: When we put on our stoles, this means that we will follow Jesus' example to love and serve others just as Jesus did.

- Invite the children to talk about the symbols on their stoles.

- Have the pastor bless the bread and the juice and celebrate Communion with the children. If the pastor is unable to be there, have a love feast instead.

- For a love feast, add platters of Bible-times foods such as cheese, grapes, dates, olives, figs, or fig cookies. Cut a pomegranate in half so that the children may taste the seeds. Pomegranates are usually available in the produce section of grocery stores.

- Say: We are tasting foods like Jesus and his friends ate in Bible times. When Jesus shared bread and juice with his friends, he asked them to remember him.

- Talk with the children about what they remember about Jesus.

- Pray: Thank you, God, for Jesus. Thank you for his great love for us. Amen.

Pray 'n Go

grocery-size paper bag for each child, bread baskets, stoles, chalices, marker

- Write the name of each child in the group on a grocery-size paper bag. Place the bags along the wall of the room. Have the children put their stoles, bread baskets, and chalices in their bags. Have the children sit on the floor.

- Say: Today we will make our prayer circle in a special way. Listen to my description of a person. When you recognize yourself, go and stand in the circle.

- Use this rhyme:

  I look at all the faces, smiling up at me.
  There is God's creation in every face I see.
  I see someone with (*Describe a child; try to use characteristics more than just appearance.*)

- When everyone is in the prayer circle, **pray: Dear God, we thank you for Jesus, who taught us to love and serve others. Help us to follow his example. Help us to remember Jesus whenever we come together for Communion. Amen.**

manger	hay
angel	teacher
brother	love
share	children

Word Cards

sick	**branches**
room	**friends**
bread	**cup**
altar	**true**

Word Cards 59

Family Retreats

The outlines for a family retreat on baptism and a family retreat on Communion may be found on pages 61-64.

Choose from the activities as your time and setting allow. Build in time for meals, snacks, recreation, and relaxation. You might have organized games for recreation or take advantage of your retreat site and enjoy canoeing, hiking, walking, skiing, bicycling, and so forth as families. Refer to the page numbers printed beside an activity for more details. Listed below are some suggested retreat schedules:

One-Day Retreat

Morning Arrival
Breakfast snack
Welcome
Session 1
Recreation
Lunch
Session 2
Snack
Session 3 *(Closing Worship)*

Overnight Retreat

Evening Arrival
Supper
Welcome
Recreation

Breakfast
Session 1
Recreation
Lunch
Session 2
Snack
Session 3 *(Closing Worship)*

Weekend Retreat

Evening Arrival
Supper
Welcome
Recreation

Breakfast
Session 1
Recreation
Lunch
Recreation
Snack
Recreation
Supper
Session 2

Breakfast
Session 3 *(Closing Worship)*

© 1994 Cokesbury.

Baptism Retreat

God said, "You are my own dear Son. I am pleased with you."
(Mark 1:11, Good News Bible, adapted)

Session 1

Gathering
- Make Nametags (see "Who's Who," page 6)
- Play the "Water Works" game (see page 6)
- Sing "Tell Me the Stories of Jesus " (see "Sing 'n Swing," page 7) and "Drip, Drop, Splish, Splash" (see "Splash 'n Sing," page 8, and page 14).

Family Discussion
- Have everyone sit in family groups. Make sure everyone is invited into a group. Photocopy the Baptism Information Questionnaire (page 13) for each person. You may want to send this to participants before the retreat, but be sure to have copies available at the retreat. Talk about the questions on the information questionnaire. If someone in the family groups has not been baptized, have that person remember someone he or she knows who has been baptized.

Bible Story
- Read the story of Jesus' baptism from Matthew 3:13-17 and Mark 1:9-11.

Bible Verse
- Say the Bible verse, "God said, 'You are my own dear Son. I am pleased with you'" (Mark 1:11, Good News Bible, adapted).
- Play the Bible verse game "Touch the Water" (page 7).

Activity Time
- Talk about some of the symbols for baptism. Baptism symbols include:
  1. **Water**. Water is necessary for life. At baptism water symbolizes the new life we have in Jesus. Water also symbolizes cleansing. We wash our bodies, our dishes, our clothes, and even our pets with water. At baptism water symbolizes the cleansing of our sin.
  2. **Dove.** The Scriptures tell us that when Jesus was baptized, he saw a dove and heard God's voice. The dove is the symbol for the Holy Spirit.
  3. **Shell.** The shell with three drops of water symbolizes our baptism into the body of Christ in the name of the Father, the Son, and the Holy Spirit.

- Have each participant make a baptism cross. Prepare simple wooden crosses before the retreat. Use thin wood and make the crosses about eight inches long and five inches wide.

- Have each person use a wood burner or a permanent marker to burn or write the date of his or her baptism on the cross. **Always have adult supervision when using a wood burner.** If participants do not know the date of their baptism, or have not been baptized, have them move on to the next step.

- Let the participants glue shells and pearls onto their crosses however they wish.

- If you cannot prepare the wooden crosses, purchase small wooden plaques or cut pieces of cardboard into eight-by-seven-inch plaques. Let the participants glue the shells onto plaques in the shape of a cross. Have participants burn or write their baptism dates on the plaques.

- You may order balsa wood strips, shells, pearls, wooden plaques, and wood burners from:
  S & S
  1-800-243-9232

Watch a Video
- Show the Jesus' baptism portion of the *Jesus of Nazareth* video. This is found on Tape 1, one hour, thirty-eight minutes into the tape. This portion lasts about five minutes. This video is available from Cokesbury ICN 475309.

Prayer
- Close with the "Sing a Blessing" activity (page 9).

Session 2

Gathering
- Sing "Tell Me the Stories of Jesus " (see "Sing 'n Swing," page 7), "Drip, Drop, Splish, Splash" (see "Splash 'n Sing," page 8, and page 14) and "If You're Happy and You Know It." Sing the new words printed on page 62.

If you know you're God's creation,
  Clap your hands. *(Clap, clap.)*
If you know you're God's creation,
  Clap your hands. *(Clap, clap.)*
If you know you're God's creation,
  Just like every race and nation,
If you know you're God's creation,
  Clap your hands. *(Clap, clap.)*

If you know that Christ's your brother,
  Clap your hands. *(Clap, clap.)*
If you know that Christ's your brother,
  Clap your hands. *(Clap, clap.)*
If you know that Christ's your brother,
  And he loves you like no other,
If you know that Christ's your brother,
  Clap your hands. *(Clap, clap.)*

If you know the Holy Spirit,
Clap your hands. *(Clap, clap.)*
If you know the Holy Spirit,
Clap your hands. *(Clap, clap.)*
If you know the Holy Spirit,
Don't just sit there, now, let's hear it!
If you know the Holy Spirit,
Clap your hands. *(Clap, clap.)*

Words: James Ritchie, © 1997 James Ritchie.

Family Discussion
- Have everyone sit in family groups. Have copies of *The United Methodist Hymnal* available. Look at the services for the Baptismal Covenants beginning on page 33. **What words remind us of the baptism of Jesus? What words were said by the pastor? By the person receiving baptism or by the parents of the child being baptized? What words were said by the congregation?**

Bible Story
- Tell the story "Jesus Is God's Son" *(page 5)*. Do the actions suggested in the "Hand 'n Hand Bible Story" activity *(page 7)*.

Bible Verse
- Say the Bible verse, "God said, 'You are my own dear Son. I am pleased with you'" (Mark 1:11, *Good News Bible*, adapted).

- Play the Bible verse game "Dove Hunt" *(page 27)*.

Activity Time
- Divide the group into two work teams.
  Team One: Bake "Dove Delights" cookies *(see page 18)*.
  Team Two: Make baptism gifts for babies in your congregation. Provide white handkerchiefs or cut white fabric into 12-inch squares. Photocopy the dove pattern *(page 60)*. Let the families make stencils by cutting the patterns out of paper plates or file folders.

- Cover the work area with rolled paper (newspapers will rub ink onto the white fabric). Stretch the handkerchief or fabric out flat and secure with tape. Tape the stencil on top of the handkerchief or fabric. Pour stencil paint onto inexpensive paper plates. Show the participants how to dip stencil brushes into the paint, wipe excess paint off onto the paper plate, and then brush over the stencil onto the fabric. Let the stencils dry.

- You may order stencil paints and stencil brushes from:

  S & S
  1-800-243-9232

- Plan to save the stenciled handkerchiefs to give as baptism keepsakes to infants baptized in your church.

Watch a Video
- Show the Jesus' baptism portion of *The Gospel According to Matthew* video. This is found on Tape 1, Matthew 3:1-17. This video is available from Cokesbury ICN 807685.

- Enjoy eating the "Dove Delights" while watching the video.

Prayer
- Close with the "Sing a Blessing" activity *(page 9)*.

Session 3

Family Discussion
- Read the congregational pledges from page 44 of *The United Methodist Hymnal*. Have each family make a list of things they do or can do to help fulfill the promise the congregation makes at baptisms.

Think About Baptism
- Invite the pastor to talk about baptism. Perhaps the pastor might begin by telling the story of her or his own baptism. Use these questions as a guideline: **Who can be baptized? Why do we use a baptismal font? What are the different ways people can be baptized? What does it mean to reaffirm your baptism?**

Prepare the Worship Space
- Play "Water Sounds" from the **CD.**
- Prepare a pitcher of water and a baptismal bowl or font.
- Set up chairs or seats for participants.

Remember Your Baptism
- Have your pastor lead the group in the "Congregational Reaffirmation of the Baptismal Covenant" found in *The United Methodist Hymnal* beginning on page 50.

Communion Retreats

Do this in memory of me.
(Luke 22:19, *Good News Bible*)

Session 1

Gathering
- Make Nametags (*see "Who's Who," page 35*).
- Play the "Remember Game" (*see page 35*).
- Sing "HA-le-lu-jah!" (*see "Sing 'n Swing," page 45, and page 51*) and "We Can Remember" (*see "Sing 'n Remember," page 36, and page 41*).

Family Discussion
- Have everyone sit in family groups. Make sure everyone is invited into a group. Talk about mealtimes. **Does your family do anything special at mealtime? Who says the blessing? Do you eat at about the same time each day? Do you eat at the same place for each meal? Who sets the table? What important times in our lives include special meals?** (*holidays, birthdays, weddings, funerals, Mother's Day, confirmation*) **Why do you think we want to eat when we celebrate special occasions? What are some important meals that you have enjoyed at church? Name the times the church family eats together.**

Bible Story
- Tell the story of the Passover from Exodus 12.

- During Passover Jewish people remember how God saved their ancestors from slavery in Egypt. God told Moses that the Hebrews should celebrate the Festival of Unleavened Bread to remember the Passover. Today at Passover Jewish people still have a Seder meal, at which time special foods are eaten to remember the event. Jesus was in Jerusalem at Passover, and it was at this special supper Jesus had with his disciples that he gave them the bread to represent his body and a cup to represent his blood. We remember this Last Supper when we celebrate Holy Communion today.

© 1991 Cokesbury.

Bible Verse
- Say the Bible verse, "Do this is memory of me" (Luke 22:19, *Good News Bible*).
- Play the game "Grape Jam Bible Verse" (*page 37*).

Activity Time
- Prepare Passover foods to taste. Tell the meaning of each food. If you're planning a complete Passover meal, or Seder, invite a rabbi to conduct the meal.

- Passover foods include:
  1. **Roasted lamb**. Roast lamb bones prior to the retreat. Cut the roasted lamb into small pieces.
  2. **Eggs**. Hardboil the eggs.
  3. **Green herbs**. Separate parsley into small pieces.
  4. **Bitter herbs**. Separate romaine lettuce, endive, and/or horseradish into small pieces.
  5. **Matzo**. Purchase matzo crackers.
  6. **Charoset**. Make charoset (see below).

Charoset
6 apples
4 tablespoons grape juice
½ teaspoon cinnamon
⅔ cup chopped pecans or walnuts
3 tablespoons sugar
grated rind of 1 lemon

Peel and core apples. Slice the apples and place them in a food processor. Chop finely. Place apples in a large bowl. Add other ingredients until the mixture looks like coarse applesauce.

- Explain the significance of each food.
  1. **Roasted lamb.** The symbol of the lamb's blood painted on the doorposts when the angel of death passed over the Hebrews' homes.
  2. **Eggs.** A symbol of life.
  3. **Green herbs.** A symbol of spring.
  4. **Bitter herbs.** A symbol of the bitter and hard life the Hebrews had as slaves in Egypt.
  5. **Matzo.** A reminder that the Hebrews left Egypt in a hurry and did not have time to let the bread rise.
  6. **Charoset.** The symbol of the bricks made by the Hebrew slaves.

Watch a Video
- Show *The Ten Commandments* video or the TNT *Moses* video, at least the portion about Passover (available from Gospel Films, Inc., 1-800-253-0413).

Prayer
- Close the session with prayer.

Session 2

Gathering
• Sing "HA-le-lu-jah!" (see "Sing 'n Swing," page 45, and page 51) and "We Can Remember" (see "Sing 'n Remember," page 36, and page 41).

Family Discussion
• Have everyone sit in family groups. Recall some of your favorite meals with your closest friends. **What are some things you did to make sure the meals were special? What happened during those meals that caused you to remember that time together? Does eating a particular food make you think of someone? Why?**

Bible Story
• Review the events leading up to the Last Supper. Remind the group that Jesus was going to Jerusalem for the Passover.

• Read Matthew 26:17-29 and Luke 22:7-20. Ask the families to listen for differences in the two accounts of the Last Supper.

• Talk about how Jesus used the important celebration of the Passover meal to give his disciples new meaning for an old tradition. Draw parallels between the symbols of Passover and the symbols of the Last Supper.
The Lamb. At Passover the lamb was sacrificed so the blood could be used to mark the doorways. Jesus is called the Lamb of God. Jesus died on the cross so that we might have eternal life.
The Deliverer. Moses was called the Deliverer because he was chosen by God to save God's people. Jesus is the Messiah, the chosen one, who delivers all who believe in him.
Bread and wine. Both meals use the bread and wine as symbols to help us remember important events of faith and of God's work.

Bible Verse
• Say the Bible verse, "Do this is memory of me" (Luke 22:19, Good News Bible).
• Play the game "Bible Verse Jumble" (pages 46 and 49).

Activity Time
• Divide the group into three work teams.
Team One: Bake bread for Communion (see page 56).
Team Two: Make a worship cloth. Provide white fabric or a flat sheet, markers, and symbol patterns (page 40). Let the families trace the patterns on the cloth. Use the markers to color in the symbols.

Team Three: Create a Litany of Thanksgiving to be used in the celebration of Communion.

Watch a Video
• Show the Last Supper portion of the Jesus of Nazareth video. This is found on Tape 3, about forty-one minutes into the tape. This portion lasts about twelve minutes. This video is available from Cokesbury ICN 475309.

Prayer
• Close the session with prayer.

Session 3

Family Discussion
• Have each family make a chart on a large piece of paper. Write the words, "When we think about you, Jesus, we remember . . . ." Have each group write as many things as they can think of to complete the sentence.

Think About Holy Communion
• Invite the pastor to talk about Holy Communion. Use these questions as a guideline: **What are those words we say, read, or hear, and what do they mean? What are the elements? Why do we use bread and juice? Who fixes them for us? What does it mean to consecrate the elements? Can anyone consecrate the elements? What happens to the leftovers? Can anyone serve Communion? Why is the altar covered with a white cloth?**

• Remind the group that the Passover was celebrated by Jesus and transformed into our celebration of Holy Communion. Emphasize remembering.

Prepare the Worship Space
• Play "Let Us Break Bread Together" from the **CD.**
• Prepare the bread and juice.
• Place the cloth on the altar.
• Set up chairs or seats for participants.
• Display the words to the Litany of Thanksgiving.

Celebrate Communion
• Have your pastor lead the group in the celebration of Communion. Include the Litany of Thanksgiving.